Stalin and Stalinism

SECOND EDITION

MARTIN McCAULEY

LONGMAN
LONDON AND NEW YORK

Addison Wesley Longman Limited
Edinburgh Gate, Harlow
Essex CM20 2JE, England
and Associated Companies throughout the world.

*Published in the United States of America
by Addison Wesley Longman Inc., New York*

First published 1983
Tenth impression 1990
Second edition 1995
Second impression 1996

ISBN 0 582 27658 6 PPR

British Library Cataloguing-in-Publication Data

A catalogue record for this book is
available from the British Library

Library of Congress Cataloging-in-Publication Data

McCauley, Martin.
    Stalin and Stalinism / Martin McCauley. -- 2nd ed.
        p. cm. -- (Seminar Studies in history)
    Includes bibliographical references and index.
    ISBN 0-582-27658-6 (paper)
    1. Soviet Union-- Politics and government--1917–1936. 2. Soviet
Union--Politics and government-- 1936–1953. 3. Stalin, Jospeh,
1879–1953. I. Title. II. Series.
DK267.M39 1995
947.084'2--dc20   95-10104
                                                                    CIP

Set by 7 in 10/12 Sabon Roman
Produced through Longman Malaysia, GPS

HISTORY DEP

Don
£7.99

on file

5

STALIN AND STALINISM

CONTENTS

EDITORIAL FOREWORD

Such is the pace of historical enquiry in the modern world that there is an ever-widening gap between the specialist article or monograph, incorporating the results of current research, and general surveys, which inevitably become out of date. *Seminar Studies in History* are designed to bridge this gap. The books are written by experts in their field who are not only familiar with the latest research but have often contributed to it. They are frequently revised in order to take account of new information and interpretations. They provide a selection of documents to illustrate major themes and provoke discussion, and also a guide to further reading. Their aim is to clarify complex issues without over-simplifying them, and to stimulate readers into deepening their knowledge and understanding of major themes and topics.

ROGER LOCKYER

NOTE ON REFERENCING SYSTEM

Readers should note that numbers in square brackets [5] refer them to the corresponding entry in the Bibliography at the end of the book (specific page references are given in italic). A number in square brackets preceded by *Doc*. [*Doc*. 5] refers readers to the corresponding item in the Document section which follows the main text. Words and abbreviations asterisked at first occurrence are defined in the Glossary.

ACKNOWLEDGEMENTS

The publishers would like to thank the following for permission to reproduce copyright material: HarperCollins Publishers Limited and Scribner, an imprint of Simon & Schuster, Inc., for a number of extracts from Nadezhda Mandelstam, *Hope against Hope*, translated from the Russian by Max Hayward. Copyright © 1970 by Atheneum Publishers; English translation copyright © by Atheneum Publishers. Milovan Djilas and Harcourt Brace & Company for two extracts from Milovan Djilas, *Conversations with Stalin*. The *Financial Times* for extracts from a report by Chrystia Freeland, © *Financial Times* 13–14 August 1994. *Europe-Asia Studies* for a table from M. Ellman and S. Maksudov's article, 'Soviet Deaths in the Great Patriotic War: a note' vol. 46, no. 4, 1994; and for a table from M. Harrison's article 'Soviet Economic Growth since 1928: the alternative statistics of G.I. Khanin' vol. 45, no. 1, 1993. Macmillan Press Ltd for a table from E. Zaleski, *Stalinist Planning for Economic Growth 1933–1952* (1980).

Although every effort has been made we have been unable to trace the copyright holders of an extract from *Soviet Foreign Policy During the Patriotic War* and *Tito Speaks* by V. Dedijer and would appreciate any information that would enable us to do so.

FOREWORD TO THE SECOND EDITION

The demise of the Soviet Union revealed one truth about Stalinism: it was flawed and its internal contradictions led to its own destruction. However, elements of this extraordinary phenomenon survive in post-1991 Russia and provide inspiration to many communists. Scholarly research on Stalin and Stalinism has expanded rapidly since the first edition of this study. The formerly dominant totalitarian interpretation began to be undermined in the 1960s, but it was only in the 1980s, with a new generation of scholars known as the 'new cohort' or 'social historians', that a coherent, alternative school of thought emerged. Sheila Fitzpatrick is the leading light in this constellation and she has stimulated a vigorous debate. Totalitarians concentrate on the state and ideology, and Stalin is central to their deliberations. The new cohort regard this as politics from above and choose to research politics from below. They search out groups which benefited from the policies of the period, thus arguing that Stalinism had its social as well as political dynamic. They do not seek to link their studies to the overall political scene. A major point of controversy between the totalitarians and the social historians is the terror. The former regard it as deliberately orchestrated from above, the latter as evidence of chaos and the ungovernability of the state, with much of the terror originating at the local level. The Stalinist state, in the end, could not be reformed. When Gorbachev tried to introduce a social democratic Union of Sovereign States he merely hastened its demise.

Scholarly thinking about Stalin and Stalinism is at present negative. No major scholar has come out with a defence of the Stalin phenomenon. Perhaps one will emerge in the future, but in order to vindicate Stalin one needs to suspend moral judgment. However, it would be naive to blame one leader for the travails of his country. Scholars now need to identify what was unique about Stalin and Stalinism, separating them from the Russian or Soviet context in which they operated. To do this one needs to understand how the Stalinist state operated in practice. Stalinist studies are only in their infancy.

MARTIN MCCAULEY

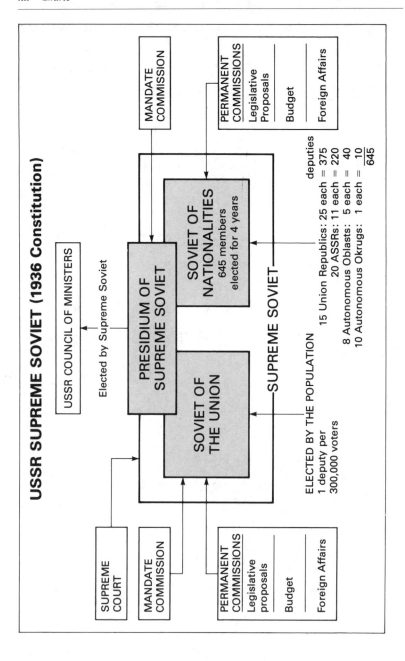

USSR SUPREME SOVIET (1936 Constitution)

MANDATE COMMISSION

PERMANENT COMMISSIONS
Legislative Proposals

Budget

Foreign Affairs

USSR COUNCIL OF MINISTERS

Elected by Supreme Soviet

PRESIDIUM OF SUPREME SOVIET

SOVIET OF NATIONALITIES
645 members
elected for 4 years

SOVIET OF THE UNION

SUPREME SOVIET

ELECTED BY THE POPULATION
1 deputy per
300,000 voters

15 Union Republics: 25 each = 375
20 ASSRs: 11 each = 220
8 Autonomous Oblasts: 5 each = 40
10 Autonomous Okrugs: 1 each = 10
                                    645   deputies

SUPREME COURT

MANDATE COMMISSION

PERMANENT COMMISSIONS
Legislative proposals

Budget

Foreign Affairs

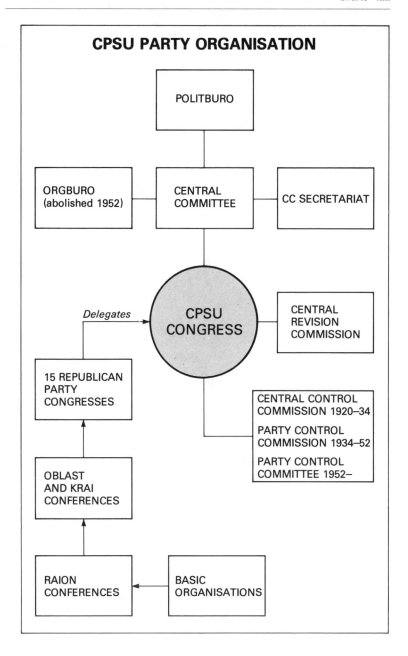

CPSU PARTY ORGANISATION

POLITBURO

ORGBURO
(abolished 1952)

CENTRAL
COMMITTEE

CC SECRETARIAT

Delegates

CPSU
CONGRESS

CENTRAL
REVISION
COMMISSION

15 REPUBLICAN
PARTY
CONGRESSES

CENTRAL CONTROL
COMMISSION 1920–34

PARTY CONTROL
COMMISSION 1934–52

PARTY CONTROL
COMMITTEE 1952–

OBLAST
AND KRAI
CONFERENCES

RAION
CONFERENCES

BASIC
ORGANISATIONS

PART ONE: THE BACKGROUND

1 THE RUSSIAN REVOLUTION AND THE SOVIET STATE, 1917–29

THE OCTOBER REVOLUTION

To the exultant Lenin the chief task after the October Revolution was the building of the 'proletarian socialist state'. However, the proletariat or working class was numerically very small (about 10 per cent of the population in 1917), there were many interpretations of socialism, and Lenin himself had declared in his *State and Revolution*, written in exile in August 1917: 'So long as the state exists there can be no freedom. When freedom exists there will be no state.' The early decrees of the Council of People's Commissars (*Sovnarkom*)* did not spell out what the Bolsheviks* understood by socialism and by the state. They were mainly devoted to institutionalising the gains of the various segments of the population which welcomed the removal of the Provisional government. October was a Soviet* revolution, a proletarian revolution, a peasant revolution and a national revolution. It was Soviet since the Bolsheviks, on taking power, had handed it over to the IInd All-Russian Congress* of Soviets of Workers' and Soldiers' Deputies. This had a Bolshevik majority and passed two important decrees – one concerning the need for an immediate peace and the other dealing with land tenure – set up *Sovnarkom*, and elected an All-Russian Central Executive Committee (CEC)* which was to act in the name of the Congress when the latter was not in session [1]. The revolution was proletarian since workers' control was instituted in industry and the working class expected that they would run the economy and be the dominant class in the state. It was a peasant revolution in that it abolished the private ownership of land, and handed over the landlords' estates to the peasants. Land could henceforth be cultivated only by those who worked it themselves; there was to be no buying, selling or leasing of land or hiring of labour. It was also a national revolution because it affected over half the population and promised non-Russians national self-determination. This implied that they could secede from the new Soviet Russian state if they so desired. When the Russian Soviet Republic was set up by the IIIrd All-Russian Congress of Soviets in January 1918 it was proclaimed as a 'free union of free nations, as a federation of Soviet national republics'.

Lenin accepted that Soviet Russia could not exist on her own, nor could she grow into a socialist state on her own. The Bolsheviks hoped that the spark of the October Revolution would ignite the flame of the international socialist revolution. This in turn would set the whole capitalist world ablaze and lead to socialism replacing capitalism as the dominant force on the stage of history.

However, Soviet Russia had inherited an unwanted legacy – war against imperial Germany and her allies. She sought desperately to end the war but her appeals to the belligerent nations went unheeded. The western Allies were appalled by the Soviet desire for a unilateral peace in the east, by the government's repudiation of Tsarist debts and by the call for worldwide revolution. Germany would only conclude peace on her terms. The issue of war or peace split the Central Committee (CC)* of the Communist Party in three factions. Lenin, ever the realist, wanted peace at any price. He was well aware that the Reds had no army; the old army had disintegrated as the soldiers left the front to claim their share of the land. The left communists,* led by Bukharin, wanted revolutionary war. To them appeals to the western Allies for aid or for the conclusion of a peace treaty with Germany were tantamount to the betrayal of the international working-class movement. The left communists believed that a revolutionary war would fire workers and peasants for the cause and so lead to the formation of a new army. Trotsky hit on a third solution, neither war nor peace. He thought that the German army was not capable of launching a new offensive, hence all that Soviet Russia had to do was to sit it out until the socialist revolution in Germany swept away the Kaiser. Unfortunately, Trotsky's assessment of German military might was totally incorrect and the German forces moved forward at will – indeed they could have occupied the whole of the country had they so desired. However, the German government calculated that it stood to gain more by reaching a negotiated settlement and since Lenin's faction had gained a majority in the CC a peace treaty was signed at Brest-Litovsk* on 3 March 1918. The left communists' conviction that such a move was a mistake was mirrored by some officials in the German foreign ministry who would have preferred Germany not to have recognised Soviet Russia. This would have given Germany a free hand, since as far as Berlin was concerned Soviet Russia did not exist in international law.

Peace with Germany did not mean that the danger of an armed overthrow of Bolshevik power had disappeared. On 23 February 1918 – even before Brest-Litovsk – the Red Army was founded, not to carry revolution beyond the frontiers of Soviet Russia, but to defend the gains of the revolution at home. Its moving spirit was Trotsky and he was to fashion it into a very competent fighting force. A threat to Bolshevik power materialised in the north, where the British occupied the port of Murmansk in June 1918 to ensure that the munitions there did not fall into German hands. Soon Italian, American and Serbian troops arrived as well. In the east the Czech Legion, formed of ex-prisoners of war on their way to Vladivostok to be shipped to France, seized part of the Trans-Siberian Railway. In the south there were various 'White' armies forming and Ukraine was still under German control.

The collapse of imperial Germany, the armistice of 11 November 1918, the seizure of power by revolutionaries in Bavaria and Hungary and the prospect of the whole of Germany going socialist fired the enthusiasm of the Bolsheviks and nourished their belief that the current of history was flowing in their direction. However, the capitalist powers resolved to dam it and this led to their intervention on the side of the Whites during the Civil War. Yet such was the war-weariness and home-sickness of the Interventionist forces that they rarely fired a shot in anger at the Bolsheviks, though considerable war material and diplomatic support was extended to the Whites. By the end of 1919 all foreign troops, except some American and Japanese units in Vladivostok and some British in the Crimea, had departed for home. The Americans were later to force the Japanese to abandon their position, thus facilitating Soviet control over the Far East.

Therefore 1919 was the turning point. At one time during that year it appeared that with White troops under Admiral Kolchak moving westwards from Siberia, others commanded by General Denikin moving up from Ukraine and penetrating to Orel (about 300 kilometres south-west of Moscow, the new capital), and General Yudenich poised outside Petrograd, the tables were about to be turned on the Reds. Nevertheless the Whites failed to score a decisive victory and disintegrated quickly thereafter.

To Lenin, Europe in 1919 was pregnant with revolution. In his 'April Theses', proclaimed on his return to Petrograd from exile in Switzerland in 1917, he had proposed the foundation of a new

International. This was to replace the Second International which he regarded as having betrayed the working class by supporting war in 1914. The founding meeting of the Communist International (Comintern)* took place in Moscow in March 1919 but could only muster fifty-two delegates, many of them resident in Soviet Russia. It was the second Congress, convened in Petrograd on 19 July 1920 and later moved to Moscow, which was decisive. Over 200 delegates were present and they passed the twenty-one conditions of membership drafted by Lenin. All parties wishing to join the Comintern had to be called communist parties and break with social democracy. Democratic centralism was to be practised. Their first loyalty was to be to Soviet Russia and they were to give unconditional aid to any Soviet republic. All resolutions of the Executive Committee of the Communist International were to be binding. On the face of it an international organisation had come into being, the goal of which was to promote world socialist revolution. In reality, the true beneficiary was the All-Russian Communist Party (RCP).* The failure of socialists elsewhere to seize and hold power and the fact that the second Congress met at a time when the Red Army was routing the Poles, who had invaded Ukraine in April 1920, reinforced the dominance of the RCP. Whereas at the first Congress the Bolsheviks expected Berlin to become the socialist capital of Europe, in 1920 Moscow was beginning to take on this role.

The victorious Reds faced a dilemma when they reached the Polish frontier: should they stop and sign an armistice or should they continue and carry revolution to the centre of Europe? Lenin had no doubts, but Trotsky did not share his optimism. The Polish leader Pilsudski called for a national uprising and the workers rallied to the defence of their fatherland. They shared their compatriots' view of the invading army as the Russian bear, hungry once again for Polish territory, and not as the liberating arm of the Third International. The 'miracle of the Vistula' (the Polish victory) was due mostly to Polish resistance but a contributory factor was the lack of coordination in Red Army ranks, for which Stalin must take some of the blame. An armistice was signed on 12 October 1920, shifting the frontier considerably further to the east of the old one, the Curzon line. The peace treaty was concluded at Riga on 18 March 1921.

After their defeat at Warsaw, the communists changed some of their attitudes. There was plainly not going to be a revolution in the west and the lack of enthusiasm displayed by the Polish workers towards the extension of Soviet power was probably shared by the rest of the European working class. Until August 1920 the Bolsheviks had paid little attention to frontiers: theirs was a state in constant flux. Now it was of paramount importance to stake out the frontiers of the new order. The People's Commissariat of Foreign Affairs suddenly became important as the communists sought to conclude treaties with all contiguous states. National self-determination had resulted in Finland, Latvia, Lithuania, Estonia and Poland slipping away. Lenin was taken aback by the number of nationalities which were trying to leave, first and foremost Ukraine and Georgia. Did national self-determination mean that the entire population of a territory had the right to decide whether to remain an integral part of Soviet Russia? Many Bolsheviks heartily disagreed with the whole policy and wanted to restrict the decision to workers. 'No', said Lenin, 'this would mean workers' self-determination and not national self-determination.' However, Lenin postulated three stages. As long as the state was at the pre-bourgeois stage of development the whole population could decide and the nation could secede. After the bourgeois revolution a socialist republic would be set up by the workers in the part of the country they dominated. Finally, when its Communist Party felt strong enough, the socialist republic could apply for admission to the Soviet Russian federal state. This was the theory, but in practice the interests of the Soviet state took precedence. Moscow needed the industrial and agrarian riches of Ukraine, it could not tolerate a Menshevik*-ruled Georgia, and if other nationalities were permitted to secede they might join the camp of the adversary.

Did Soviet Russia see herself as a revolutionary base or as a state? Liberal attitudes towards the question of national self-determination prevailed as long as the former assumption held sway, but by late 1920 it was apparent that the latter view had taken over.

STATE CAPITALISM AND WAR COMMUNISM*

Sovnarkom, headed by Lenin, was subordinate to the CEC. All significant decrees were to be submitted to the CEC for its approval. However, whereas *Sovnarkom* met daily and sometimes twice a day, the CEC met only five times during the first ten days of its existence and then less frequently. This led to more and more legislation bypassing the CEC. During the first year of Soviet power only sixty-eight decrees out of a total of 480 were placed before the CEC. The key role in this process was played by Yakov Sverdlov. A close confidant of Lenin, he became chairman of the CEC on 21 November 1917. As the Presidium* (the ruling group) of the CEC became more powerful, Sverdlov was able to restrict debate in the full CEC. He was instrumental in getting the CEC to accept the terms of the Brest-Litovsk treaty. This decision led to the left Socialist Revolutionaries (SRs)* breaking with the Bolsheviks. They also abandoned their government posts (which they had held since December 1917) and joined the opposition. Blyumkin, a left SR, assassinated von Mirbach, the German ambassador, in an attempt to rekindle the fires of war with imperial Germany.

The Bolsheviks were now on their own and Sverdlov needed all his skill to dam the flood of opposition. The Presidium increasingly dictated to the CEC and critics were simply not given the floor. In June 1918 Mensheviks and most SRs (moderate socialists)* were accused of counter-revolutionary activities and removed from the CEC and provincial soviets. Hence by the summer of 1918 the Bolsheviks held full sway in the supreme Soviet organisation.

The soviets and not the Communist Party were the key institution until the summer of 1918. This was due to the fact that the Bolsheviks were ill-prepared for local government, and there was practically no communist party network in the countryside. The best party men went to work in the soviets, since that was where power lay. Yet the sheer profusion of soviets was their undoing. They could hardly resist Bolshevik efforts to amalgamate them – workers', peasants' and soldiers' soviets were fused into single units. When Bolshevik behaviour became blatantly partisan, Mensheviks and SR deputies would walk out, thus permitting the communists to replace the moderates with their own nominees. By the time the moderate socialists realised that this tactic was self-defeating it was too late to remedy the situation. The Bolsheviks' aim was to centralise decision-making in the soviets and by the summer of 1918 they were not far from their goal, thanks to the activities of Yakov Sverdlov in Moscow and communists at the local level. The CC of the Communist Party was undecided about what economic policy to adopt after October [8]. Lenin was well aware that Russian industrial development was in its infancy and that there were only pockets of advanced technology. The banking and financial services sector had been quite advanced in 1914 but was hampered by the backwardness of society. The egalitarian tradition of the countryside did not take easily to active money and credit. When the Bolsheviks took over, the economy was heading for collapse and inflation had ravaged the rouble. Lenin, like Trotsky, knew that workers were quite incapable of running the economy and wanted to keep industry going under its own management. The workers could be limited to supervising production. On the other hand, Bukharin and Preobrazhensky, the leading left communists, wanted the march to socialism to begin immediately. In many cases the decision was made by workers who simply took over the factories when they could and demanded that the CC nationalise them. This move was often successful on the periphery but the CC could frustrate it in the industrial heartland. However, on 28 June 1918, wholesale nationalisation was decreed. This was partly in response to these wildcat moves, but also to the approaching Civil War and to the risk that the factories might be acquired by foreign, especially German, interests. The Supreme Council of the National Economy (VSNKh),* set up in December 1917, now had a real task on its hands. The nationalisation decree can be seen as the end of the phase of state capitalism* and the beginning of war communism.

Workers' control, official Bolshevik policy as of 27 November 1917, was effected through factory committees. As the proletariat was further to the left than Lenin there were constant clashes on what workers' control actually meant. The main weakness of the factory committee was that it was restricted to one factory, but there was an All-Russian Council of Factory Committees; it in turn, however, recognised the trade unions as superior organs.

By early 1918 the Bolsheviks were in a leading position in the main industrial trade unions after successfully outmanoeuvring the Mensheviks. The latter had found themselves heading key trade unions in October 1917 – the union controlling the railways and the telegraph for instance – but their authority was gradually undermined by such tactics as the setting up of an alternative trade union which was immediately recognised by the government. With food desperately short, ration cards were handed out only to members of the approved union.

Even with trade unions controlled on paper by the Bolsheviks, it did not follow that they would carry out Lenin's directives. A.G. Shlyapnikov, the first Bolshevik Commissar for Labour, felt strongly that the unions should run the economy, and indeed this found its way into party resolutions. However, the CC and *Sovnarkom* thought that running the economy was one of their duties. Under state capitalism trade unions just about held their own, but the rigours of war communism were such that they changed from organs representing labour to organs representing management. Their chief task was to instil discipline and raise labour productivity.

This was a formidable undertaking as cold, hunger and disease disillusioned and decimated the labour force. The cities emptied, Petrograd and Moscow lost half their population, and the best cadres were sent to the front. So desperate was the situation that the IXth Party Congress decided in April 1920 that non-communist specialists were to be employed, one-man management at the factory level was to take over, and party and trade union committees were to be nominated from above and not elected from below. Things were bleak indeed.

A major reason for the débâcle was that the Bolsheviks did not control the most essential strategic product, food. The peasants were very gratified that the Bolsheviks had enacted the land decree (which had been SR policy) on the morrow of the revolution. The peasant land committees thereupon parcelled out among their members estates previously belonging to the crown, the church, the monasteries and private non-peasant owners. This led to the disappearance of the big farms which had produced food for the market.

Lenin had envisaged model or state farms being set up on the confiscated estates, with soviets of poor peasants as the natural allies of the Bolsheviks in the rural areas, but in practice neither the model farms nor the soviets of poor peasants came into being.

The land decree had been a tactical move to keep the countryside quiet while the Bolsheviks consolidated their position in the cities. It achieved this in the short run, but by the summer of 1918 the peasant had very little incentive to sell his surplus production to the state organs since the rouble, at home and abroad, was worth little more than the paper it was printed on. In order to feed the cities and the Red Army the Bolsheviks therefore set up committees of poor peasants, *kombedy*,* on 11 June 1918, with orders to 'extract grain surpluses from *kulaks** and rich people'. It was intended that most of the surplus would go to the state, and the peasants were promised 'goods of prime necessity and agricultural implements'. This system did not work: the peasants were primarily concerned with looking after their own interests and still harboured a deep suspicion of central authority. This led to the formation of workers' detachments,* composed of urban workers who did bring in the grain, the main reason being that they had machine guns to underline their authority.

The policy of favouring the poor peasant against the middle and rich peasants or *kulaks* was abandoned in December 1918, when the state sided with the middle peasant against the *kulak*, but it was all to no avail. The peasants sowed less and consumed more; villages denied the Red Army entrance, soviets voted themselves out of Soviet Russia and others killed their communist members. The honeymoon with the Bolsheviks was over; the peasants had turned their backs on Marxism.

Sovnarkom quickly established itself as the key decision-making body after the revolution. However by 1921–22 the Politburo* of the CC of the Communist Party had taken over. This was a development which Lenin viewed with some dismay, and both he and Trotsky favoured the top party organ divesting itself of some of its administrative duties [5]. This never came about, however, mainly due to Lenin's ill-health and to the inept tactics adopted by Trotsky.

Lenin was fascinated by administrative detail and devoted more attention to government than to party affairs. The Bolshevik leader, on becoming prime minister, took over the existing structure of government, and the areas of competence assigned to the various commissars* he appointed were quite traditional. This inevitably led to many practices of the old society being adopted by the new. As a Marxist, Lenin regarded control of the institutions as of paramount importance, not their structure. The demarcation line between the government, composed of Bolsheviks, and the party was always fuzzy. Matters were made worse by the right of every commissar to appeal to the CC. Stalin took a radically different view from Lenin and Trotsky about the role of *Sovnarkom* and although he was himself a commissar, he gave the party primacy over the governmental bureaucracy. One of the contributory factors in the rise of the party bureaucracy was its power to make appointments not only within the party but also in government, trade unions and soviets. Such was the pressure of work that the practice developed of commissars delegating some of their functions to deputies. This inevitably affected the standing of *Sovnarkom*: it never developed into a cabinet. When Lenin fell ill his deputies waited for him to recover or passed matters on to the Politburo. It was clear that it was only Lenin who invested *Sovnarkom* with its authority.

The destruction of the previous ruling strata produced a void between the state and the workers and peasants. Lenin's daring in taking on the task of promoting socialism from above, in an economically and educationally backward state, meant that there was grave danger of inertia, anarchy and counter-revolution surfacing. The Bolsheviks were wholly unprepared for their task and lacked the experience and technical expertise to function effectively. The Communist Party inevitably found itself assuming the management of the state, since government and local soviet agencies had their own ideas about what policies should be implemented. The peasantry, the real winners in 1917, were satisfied and wanted room to develop their own rural culture. This collided head on with the goal of the Bolsheviks, to build socialism. The Bolsheviks were very astute at accumulating authority, the right to take decisions, but they discovered that their power, the ability to implement their policies, was constrained. It was almost inevitable that they would resort to authoritarianism and physical coercion if they wished to retain control of Russia.

It was the Civil War which concentrated power in the hands of the party: the desperate political, economic and military situation meant that all resources had to be brought under central control. Democracy was the first casualty as iron discipline descended on the home front. Military methods became legitimate if they achieved results. Such was the dearth of potential officials that local leaders called on Moscow to send them reliable men. The person in the party secretariat who was responsible for finding and dispatching them was Stalin; he knew more than anyone else about party cadres and he was keenly aware of the significance of this information. He built up a file which was locked away and to which even his secretary did not have automatic access.

Dissent was endemic in the CC and the Politburo. The latter contained men of great ability and education, such as Lenin, Trotsky and Bukharin, but they split on practically every major question. One issue which almost tore the party asunder was Trotsky's plan to impose military discipline on workers in order to hasten reconstruction. This was eloquent testimony to the gulf which existed between the Bolsheviks and the proletariat. After all, the Bolsheviks claimed to be the avant-garde of the working class. It became a burning question in late 1920 when the Civil War had been won; it was only resolved at the Xth Party Congress in March 1921, when war communism was abandoned and the New Economic Policy (NEP)* was adopted. The main reason for the adoption of NEP was the revolt of the countryside against requisitioning. In Samara the SRs set up their own republic. Unless concessions were made there was a risk that the cities would go hungry. The Congress was a fateful one. During it the unthinkable occurred: sailors at Kronstadt, the reddest of the red, revolted and demanded, among other things, free elections to the soviet; the uprising was suppressed in rivers of blood and the chastened delegates turned inwards on themselves. Two opposition groups –

the Workers' Opposition, led by Shlyapnikov, which wanted to return to the goals of October, with the trade unions running industry; and the Democratic Centralists, who wanted more democracy in the party – were swept aside. Factionalism was banned; only the whole party could discuss an issue, not groups or platforms; once a party decision had been taken absolute obedience to it had to be observed. Expulsion from the party could be the punishment for infringing this rule and this applied even to members of the CC (although this was kept secret until 1924).

This momentous move, seen by Lenin as temporary until the situation stabilised, introduced Politburo infallibility. Only by adopting such measures, thought Lenin, would the party be prevailed upon to accept NEP.

NEP

NEP was a step backwards for the party. Although the leadership came to like the new policy, the rank and file never came to terms with it. Large-scale industry and public services remained nationalised and all foreign trade was still conducted by the state. It was mainly light industry which passed into the hands of the NEP men. Soviet Russia desperately needed foreign capital and was fully aware of her technological backwardness. The terrible famine of 1921–22 was the legacy of war communism, but afterwards agriculture quickly found its feet again as the peasant was allowed to sell to whomever he chose. The tax in kind, payment in grain, was introduced in March 1921, but this gave way to money taxes as the rouble stabilised and the market reasserted itself [8].

The Bolsheviks found themselves in the extraordinary position of having to rely on the countryside for survival. Lenin declared that only the 'link with the peasants' could 'save the socialist revolution in Russia until revolution had occurred in other countries'. Agricultural products were in great demand in 1922 and this pushed prices up, but the peasant was not satisfied with the range of industrial goods on offer and refused to buy. Workers lost their jobs; soon over a million were unemployed. In order to survive, the industrial trusts (groups of enterprises producing similar products) resorted to price-fixing and so successful were they that by October 1923 the situation had been reversed with a vengeance. Trotsky dubbed it the 'scissors' crisis' – the blades of agricultural and industrial prices looked like scissors – and the party became alarmed at the enormous fluctuations in prices. Before it could speak on the subject, however, Trotsky launched a scathing attack on economic policy. This was followed by a letter signed by forty-six communists – the 'platform of the forty-six' – mainly supporters of Trotsky, talking of a serious economic crisis occasioned by the incompetence of the CC [5]. This was acutely embarrassing at a time when official party policy was to encourage all peasants to expand production and afford the market economy free rein. Fortunately, a good harvest in 1923 stabilised the situation and low industrial prices increased demand. Heavy industry did not fare as well but the party was determined to invest more. By 1924 the price relationship between industrial and agricultural goods was more or less back to its 1913 level; exports rose, mostly grain, and NEP appeared to be vindicating the trust placed in it.

In May 1922 Lenin suffered his first stroke, but he appeared to be his old self again during the autumn. Another, but more severe, stroke afflicted him in December 1922. It paralysed his right side but did not affect the brain. He lost his ability to speak as a result of his third stroke, in March 1923, and thereafter vegetated until he died on 21 January 1924. After the third stroke had ended all hope of a recovery the Politburo needed to find a successor. There could never be another Lenin. Although he held no formal office, he had led the party by the power of his intellect and his personality. Nevertheless he died an anxious and saddened man.

All was not right with the party and the leader was plainly unhappy with the changes which had transformed it from a conspiratorial élitist party – there had only been about 24,000 members in February 1917 – into a mass party which contained 733,000 members in March 1921 [5]. The vast majority of these members had only a nodding acquaintance with Marxism and were quite incapable of following the subtleties of the debates among the élite. They all knew what they wanted, namely socialism, which promised to bring them everything they longed for; but how was it to be realised? Despite its numbers the party was weak. It was not in command of the country; its membership was predominantly urban, while about four persons in five lived in the countryside. No wonder Lenin was worried. He was appalled by the low level of culture in Soviet Russia, by which he meant basic literacy [5].

In an effort to improve the efficiency of the Secretariat,* Stalin was appointed Secretary-General in April 1922, with Molotov and Kuibyshev becoming secretaries. This did not make Stalin nominal head of the party, since the Secretariat did not then possess the power it was later to acquire; in 1922 the Politburo was still the key decision-making body. Lenin, Trotsky, Zinoviev, Kamenev and Bukharin all appeared to be senior to Stalin.

Two incidents sowed the seeds of doubt in Lenin's mind about the fitness of Stalin to hold high office in the party. On the issue of the foreign trade monopoly Stalin flippantly disregarded his leader's passionately held view that the monopoly had to stay. Lenin had his way in the end, overturning a CC decision by personal fiat. Since Lenin had been too ill to fight his own battles he had spoken through Trotsky, thus making it plain whom he considered to be his closest associate.

The other issue over which there was acrimonious debate concerned Stalin's home republic, Georgia. Lenin was especially concerned about the Transcaucasian republic which had been dragged back into Soviet Russia by military force in 1921. Stalin wanted Georgia to become an autonomous republic (ASSR)* in the new Soviet state called the Union of Soviet Socialist Republics (USSR)* which came into being in December 1922. The Georgians rejected this notion since, as an ASSR, they would have become part of the Russian Soviet Federated Socialist Republic (RSFSR),* directly ruled from Moscow. They wanted to become a full Soviet republic and in that way retain some of their independence. Stalin did not wish for a compromise but was determined to dictate to his compatriots. As Commissar for Nationalities he was responsible for relations with all non-Russians, about half the total population of the USSR. Lenin intervened in the furore which resulted and sided with the 'injured party', the Georgians [5]. Eventually Georgia, Armenia and Azerbaidzhan were lumped together and entered the Soviet Union as the Transcaucasian Soviet Socialist Republic. Georgia became a Soviet republic in 1936.

On 24–25 December 1922, shortly after his second stroke, Lenin was able to dictate a Letter to the Congress, known as his 'Testament'. He saw the danger of a split between Stalin and Trotsky. Stalin had concentrated 'unlimited authority' in his hands and Lenin was not sure whether he would 'always be capable of using that authority with sufficient caution'. Lenin regarded Trotsky as the ablest man in the CC but feared that he revealed 'excessive self-assurance and [had] shown excessive preoccupation with the purely administrative side of the work'. So far as Kamenev and Zinoviev were concerned, Lenin thought they were not to be blamed personally for opposing the October Revolution and he referred to Bukharin and Pyatakov as the 'most outstanding representatives' of the younger generation, although he thought that Bukharin had never fully understood the motive forces of history. 'There is something scholastic in him', wrote Lenin, but he admitted that Bukharin was considered the 'darling of the whole party'. The Georgian affair excited Lenin to write an addendum to his Testament on 4 January 1923, stating that the Secretary-General was 'too rude' and that the comrades should 'think of a way of removing Stalin from that post'. In March Lenin discovered that his wife, Nadezhda Krupskaya, had been insulted by Stalin and he immediately dictated a letter to him warning him that he would break off relations if he did not apologise [23].

The Testament should have been read to the XIIth Party Congress in 1923, but Lenin's illness, the difficult position of the party, and the criticisms of major personalities the Testament contained, led to it being kept back until the following Congress in 1924.

Another problem which exercised Lenin's mind was bureaucratism. He had a low opinion of the typical Russian bureaucrat, a 'Great Russian chauvinist ... a rascal and a tyrant', as he graphically put it. Lenin was aware that traditional Tsarist practices were becoming standard procedure in Soviet Russia and he believed that Stalin was as responsible as anyone for this.

Why did Stalin clash head on with his leader in 1922–23? Would he not have been better advised to act the obedient cohort and wait for the wounded lion to die before challenging some of his views? Not enough is known to explain Stalin's behaviour satisfactorily. His conduct does reveal that he was not the 'grey blur' of Trotsky's imagination. He had views of his own and was prepared to take considerable political risks. It may be that Stalin was so fearful that Trotsky or Zinoviev or Kamenev would steal Lenin's mantle that he lost control of himself on occasions. An unofficial triumvirate, consisting of Zinoviev, Kamenev and Stalin, had come into existence in 1922 with the express purpose of blocking Trotsky, but its members do not seem to have trusted one another very much. Stalin already controlled the party machine but the Politburo decided policy.

Trotsky, as full of eloquence as he was empty of political ability, played into the hands of the triumvirate by launching, in October 1923, a vitriolic attack on the way the party was being run. He wanted a return to 'party democracy' and an end to the bureaucratic power of the Secretariat. This was instructive, coming from a politician who had favoured the militarisation of labour and had been as dictatorial as the next man when afforded the opportunity. The CC gave him a dressing down and held him indirectly responsible for the appearance of the 'platform of the forty-six'. Trotsky was not at the CC meeting to defend himself since he was convalescing with his wife in the Causasus. Henceforth illness was to overtake him at vital moments just when his political career demanded that he should be on his mettle. His bouts of ill-health may have been of psychosomatic origin. When Lenin died, Trotsky was still in the Caucasus and missed the funeral; his rather lame excuse was that Stalin had misinformed him about the date [1].

Lenin, personally a modest man, had always resisted adulation of his person. When he encountered the term Leninism he rejected it, since he held himself to be a Marxist. Nevertheless the level of culture of party members was low and they needed to be disciplined and trained. There was a vast gulf between the culture of the party leaders and the rank and file. Since Lenin was aware that the party committed errors from time to time there could be no talk of party infallibility. If the leadership made a mistake and this was realised by the rank and file, how was the party to be put back on the rails? Lenin never discovered an answer to this vital problem. The whole weight of the party apparatus was geared to suppressing dissent and stifling discussion. This was because the party felt itself to be weak; a strong, self-confident party would have tolerated the differences of opinion.

Stalin had a finely developed sense of what party members were looking for. On the eve of Lenin's funeral, 26 January 1924, Stalin delivered a remarkable speech. The mood was sombre and many feared the future without Lenin. 'We communists are people of a special mould. We are made of special stuff', declared Stalin, and he added that there was nothing higher than the calling of a member of a party whose founder and leader was comrade Lenin. How hearts must have jumped at these words! The Secretary-General first praised party members, then he set out their duties in a Lenin litany. Members swore to be exemplary communists, to preserve the unity of the party and so on. Lenin was not buried in a grave but placed in a mausoleum where the eyes of the people could gaze upon him. The slogan 'Lenin is always with us' was born. The next move was to define Leninism in terms which were accessible to everyone. This Stalin did in the course of six lectures at Sverdlov University in Moscow and they were published in *Pravda* as 'The Foundations of Leninism'. According to Stalin, the essence of Leninism consisted of stressing revolutionary will and political activism and rejecting the views of those Marxists who emphasised the dependence of political change on the development of economic and social conditions.

Leninism also meant displaying extreme relativism when assessing social forces and values: if they served the revolution they were good; otherwise they were bad. The same relativism was also to be applied to social reforms, culture, democracy, foreign affairs, etc. The party was declared to be the main motive force of the revolution [*Doc 1*]. The inchoate, spontaneous desires of the workers had to be subordinated to the grinding will of a rigidly disciplined and centralised party, otherwise the revolution could not be saved or socialism built [43].

Stalin was not the only one who sought to define Leninism. Zinoviev provided his version and Trotsky missed the boat again by opposing the whole venture, arguing that Lenin's utterances could not be dissected in such a way. Another opponent was Krupskaya, Lenin's widow, and she could show how contrary it was to Lenin's wishes. However, the mood of the times was one of veneration. Petrograd, for instance, was renamed Leningrad by the party.

Zinoviev and Stalin approached the task of defining Lenin's legacy differently. Whereas the former placed himself on a par with Lenin, Stalin projected himself as the humble apostle and devoted follower. There were many in the Soviet Union who wanted to play the same role. Bukharin and Stalin accused Trotsky of factionalism and organising a bloc together with former Democratic Centralists and left communists, while Zinoviev came up with the formulation of 'Trotskyism' as a 'definite tendency in the Russian workers' movement'.

By the beginning of 1924 the party had slimmed down to about 350,000 members, but a recruitment campaign, the 'Lenin enrolment', which was to add about 240,000 new members, was launched after Lenin's death. The most sought-after recruits were 'workers at the bench' [5]. Since the enrolment was the responsibility of Stalin, it can be safely assumed that it was impressed on new members that absolute obedience to party directives was demanded; also their political education was in the hands of men appointed by Stalin and his associates. At the XIIIth Party Congress, in May 1924, Zinoviev repeated his charge of factionalism and called on Trotsky to 'recant'. Trotsky was only just re-elected to an enlarged CC, and was isolated in the new Politburo. During the summer Trotsky and his ally, Karl Radek, lost their places on the Comintern central committee.

The political temperature was raised by Trotsky in October 1924 when he published his *Lessons of October*. This book contained vitriolic attacks on Zinoviev and Kamenev and other 'old'

Bolsheviks for their criticism of Lenin in 1917. Since Trotsky himself had only become a Bolshevik in June 1917 and had had a long record of disagreements with Lenin, he was stirring up a hornet's nest. Kamenev riposted by writing *Lenin or Trotsky*, in which he accused Trotsky of Menshevism. He found it easy to lay bare Trotsky's record of past altercations with Lenin. A veritable flood of abuse descended on the hapless Trotsky as no communist wished his own Leninist probity to be placed in doubt. The creator of the Red Army gave up his last great government office, that of Commissar for Military and Naval Affairs, and went into the political wilderness.

The controversy over *Lessons of October* gave birth to another dispute, that about socialism in one country. Stalin seized on an article by Bukharin attacking Trotsky's theory of permanent revolution and developed the argument that Trotsky's beliefs contradicted Lenin's doctrine of proletarian revolution. Lenin, according to Stalin, had held the view that the Soviet Union by herself could build socialism, but that the final victory of socialism would have to wait for revolution in several of the advanced capitalist countries. This overturned existing party assumptions that socialism in the USSR could only be built after the socialist revolution had triumphed abroad. Stalin neatly reversed the situation. Now the Soviet Union could become the pace-setter and not have to wait on world events. It was a great psychological shot in the arm for the party and the nation.

Although the 1924 harvest was a fair one, the grain did not flow into the cities. This unexpected development led to price rises, and the terms of trade turned to the advantage of the peasant. As it happened, official policy was also in favour of the peasant and in April 1925 the party announced new concessions. There were clouds on the horizon, however. In July 1924 Evgeny Preobrazhensky, a leading party economist, had argued that 'primitive socialist accumulation' – in plain language the squeezing of the peasant – was the only source of the much needed capital for industrialisation. Bukharin, however, came out with a sturdy defence of official policy and in April 1925 went even further and encouraged the peasants to enrich themselves, stating that they had nothing to fear from the authorities [17].

The situation after the excellent 1925 harvest added fuel to the flames. Again prices rose as the producers kept back grain, for they had little incentive to convert stocks into mounds of paper money which might depreciate. The agricultural tax had been reduced and this relieved the pressure of taxation. Anyway there were few quality goods to buy.

Zinoviev and Kamenev now abandoned their previous position and came out against the peasant. One of their targets was Bukharin, but Zinoviev also produced a stinging condemnation of the concept of socialism in one country. Zinoviev, as head of the Leningrad organisation, and Kamenev, as head of the Moscow party, presided over the two most important industrial cities in the country. Favouring the worker and industrialisation and opposing the peasant was natural there. However, there was more to it than this. Zinoviev, who had always regarded himself as the chief member of the triumvirate, was making his bid for leadership now that the bogey of Trotsky had been dispelled. Stalin, in turn, used his command of the party machine to telling effect at the XIVth Congress in December 1925. The Leningrad delegation was isolated as the official line was endorsed by 559 votes to 65. Zinoviev was replaced in Leningrad by Sergei Kirov. The defeat of Zinoviev also meant the political demise of Kamenev. Which direction would the victorious Stalin now take?

There were now a number of leading Bolsheviks who harboured a grudge against the leadership. In July 1926 Trotsky, Kamenev, Zinoviev, Krupskaya and nine others combined to pen the 'declaration of the thirteen', a condemnation of 'rightist' economic policy and the elimination of free debate which, to the signatories, foreshadowed the degeneration of the revolution. The CC thereupon removed Zinoviev from the Politburo and Kamenev from his remaining governmental post. The United Opposition* then attempted to take their case to the factories. At a stormy Politburo meeting in late October 1926, Trotsky depicted Stalin as the gravedigger of the revolution. This meant a parting of the ways as everyone understood that the breach was final. At the XVth Party Conference* in October–November Stalin and Bukharin poured vitriol on the United Opposition. Trotsky made his last speech to the party and was heard in silence. Kamenev was repeatedly interrupted and Zinoviev mercilessly heckled. Soon afterwards Bukharin replaced Zinoviev as chairman of the Comintern.

Foreign affairs, however, provided a stick with which to continue beating the leadership [50]. In China, disaster overtook the Comintern policy of entering into a tactical alliance with Chiang Kai-shek's Kuomintang, for in April 1927 Chiang turned his forces against the communists in Shanghai and massacred them. Then the Soviet Embassy was raided and diplomatic relations broken off.

Across the world in London, Arcos, the All-Russian Co-operative Society, was raided by the British police, and this too led to diplomatic relations being severed [5]. There were rumours of impending war. With the leadership reeling from these setbacks, a document known as the *Declaration of the 83*, chiefly drafted by Trotsky, was launched. It pulled no punches. But the leadership turned the tables on Trotsky by accusing him of treason after he had been manoeuvred into stating that unless certain changes were made he was not prepared to commit himself completely to the defence of the country. During the summer the United Opposition was pilloried in increasingly violent language but there was no legal way in which it could answer its critics, for the main organs of information were controlled by the party machine. When the opposition leaders presented a memorandum to the CC and demanded that it should be printed in preparation for the XVth Party Congress in December 1927, the request was brushed aside. They tried to print it illegally, but the political police located it and all those involved were expelled from the party. In desperation Trotsky and Zinoviev took to the streets of Moscow and Leningrad on the tenth anniversary of the revolution to proclaim their opposition. The CC responded by expelling Trotsky and Zinoviev from the party while Kamenev and some others were deprived of their seats on the CC. At the XVth Congress there was another purge. Trotsky and his closest supporters were dispatched to Alma Ata, on the Chinese frontier – in those days the back of beyond – yet even there he carried on a lively correspondence with oppositionists, so eventually, in 1929, he was deported to Turkey [1].

The 1927 harvest was satisfactory but the grain did not flow into the cities as expected; the better-off peasants preferred to build up stocks. The grain crisis predicted by the United Opposition came to pass but it was a year too late from their point of view. The Communist Party thereupon went over to the offensive and between January and March 1928 large quantities of grain were forcibly requisitioned. This led to Bukharin, Rykov and Tomsky forming the core of a new opposition group, the Right Opposition.* They wanted an end to the use of force, a better deal for the peasants and a less headlong rush into industrialisation [17]. The government began to pay more for grain but the private market price was still higher, and the winter of 1928–29 saw frequent bread shortages in Moscow and Leningrad.

The defeat of the United Opposition removed any inhibitions Stalin and his supporters may have had about stepping up industrialisation. With Trotsky out of the way, the party could engage in a U-turn away from the peasant. The new course came as a surprise to Trotsky, who had predicted a veering to the right in 1928. Many former oppositionists were favourably impressed, for Stalin was now doing what they had previously advocated. The rapid industrialisers had the wind in their sails, and the annual wrangle over grain requisitions strengthened their resolve to deal with the *kulaks* once and for all. Stalin deliberately exaggerated the danger from the right [*Doc. 2*] and went so far as to claim that Bukharin and his supporters were betraying the working class and the revolution. If anyone refused to fight the right then he too, declared Stalin, was a traitor. Bukharin desperately tried to link up with Kamenev, but the latter was a spent force. He expressed his views in *Notes of an Economist* in September 1928, but this merely provided raw material for the Stalinist propaganda machine to devour. Stalin's victory was confirmed in January 1929 when Bukharin, Rykov and Tomsky resigned from the Politburo and forfeited their state offices as well [17].

The first Five-Year Plan was adopted at a party conference in April 1929. It had been drafted in two variants, the basic and the optimum. The latter was approved, even though it was wildly optimistic and reflected the prevailing euphoria that the sky was the limit as far as industry was concerned [8]. It now became the fulcrum of Soviet activity and all other aspects of life were linked to it.

The plan set the relatively modest target of bringing 20 per cent of the sown area under the control of collectives within five years. Entry to these collective farms, or *kolkhozes*,* was to be voluntary. At the same time state farms, or *sovkhozes*,* were to be expanded, particularly in areas of virgin land, where they were to be very large.

The cult of Stalin's personality dates from 21 December 1929 when his fiftieth birthday was celebrated amid mountains of effusive prose. The leader had at last emerged openly on to the stage. Nevertheless he still did not have the authority over other persons' lives which he was to acquire in the course of the 1930s. Some of his cohorts did not regard themselves as eternal second-rank figures. It was only in 1936 that he became politically unassailable.

The party machine was Stalin's power base. The great majority of lower and middle-ranking officials were Stalin nominees. Areas outside his control were incorporated one by one: the youth organisation (the *Komsomol*),* then Leningrad, then Moscow. As the state became stronger so it became the prerogative of the centre to fill more and more posts. A nomenclature system developed which gave the party the final say in every important appointment. Lacking skill and experience the Stalinist appointees became more and more abrasive. Bluster and abuse were their only answer to criticism. The rough and often violent treatment of the peasants during the grain requisitioning of 1928 and 1929 paved the way for what was to come later. The campaigns against Trotsky, the United Opposition and the Right Opposition afforded full scope to ambitious men to demonstrate their loyalty to the party leadership. An additional spur was that if the oppositionists were defeated there would be more plum jobs to fill. Since life was often hard, the privileges and perquisites of office were eagerly sought. This form of behaviour was not restricted to party and state affairs, but extended to other facets of life, including culture. In this field battles were waged throughout the 1920s between those who believed that writers and artists should devote their talents to furthering the proletarian cause and those who regarded art as being above party politics. The All-Russian Association of Proletarian Writers (RAPP),* formed in 1928, actively invited party intervention in literature, believing it could only help their members. They discovered too late that their goals were not those of the party leadership.

Stalin was not the ostensible leader of any faction. He always played the role of the moderate and this lulled many into misjudging him. He has frequently been accused of having no ideas of his own, of being a parasite who needed a host on whom to live. At Politburo meetings during the early 1920s he often spoke last and then it was to chart a *via media* between the extremes of his more eloquent colleagues. He was instinctively on the left but could not adopt this position until Trotsky and the United Opposition had been rendered impotent. He was a very skilful politician who had a superb grasp of tactics, could predict behaviour extremely well and had an unerring eye for personal weaknesses. He floated into and out of alliances, since he had no sense of personal loyalty to any of his colleagues, and would turn on anyone if he judged it politically opportune. This personal ruthlessness served him well.

Stalin's attitude to ideas was utilitarian. If they served to make the Soviet Union stronger they were welcome. His incursion into ideology after Lenin's death served two purposes: to provide a simple, accessible exegesis of Marxism–Leninism, and to outmanoeuvre his opponents. All the issues taken up by Stalin served a practical purpose, for he was not interested in ideology as such. Industrialisation and collectivisation,* said Stalin, amounted to the revolution from above. It did not concern him that orthodox Marxism required the working class to be the agent of revolution, and that it should therefore have come from below.

Stalin was greatly assisted by the inept tactics of his opponents. Trotsky, the most formidable intellectually, was a broken reed after Lenin's death. His attacks on the party and state bureaucracy merely served to weld these groups more closely around Stalin in defence of their own positions at a time when alternative employment was hard to find. The gulf between the left and the right, in fact, was never wide; it was only Stalin's skilful manoeuvring that made it appear so. All Bolsheviks agreed that socialism entailed industrialisation. The argument between the left and the right was about the pace at which this should go ahead [8]. The left wanted rapid growth – by which they simply meant growth rates above those being achieved at the time – while the right would have been satisfied with moderate growth. The left was ready to subordinate everything to the achievement of a predetermined target, say 10 per cent annual industrial growth. The money for this would have been found by squeezing the peasants through heavy taxation, and anything which aided the fulfilment of the plan was regarded as legitimate. The right, on the other hand, looked at the economy as something that should grow organically, with industry and agriculture in tandem. Both factions regarded socialist or cooperative agriculture as the goal, but whereas the left was unwilling to allow the peasant to dictate the speed of economic growth (four out of five persons lived in the countryside) the right thought that coercion would force the peasant into resistance and would be economically disastrous. Bukharin, the main economic theorist on the right, hoped that the peasants would gradually come to see that cooperative agriculture was in their best interests. In prospering they would buy more industrial goods, thus stimulating industrial expansion [17]. Neither Trotsky nor Preobrazhensky, the main economic thinker on the left, envisaged forced collectivisation. Stalin's recourse to this was closely linked to his drive for industrialisation. He and his supporters adopted growth rates which far surpassed the demands of the left. This meant extra labour for industry and guaranteed food supplies at the expense of the countryside. So miserable were living standards in the rural areas after 1930 that peasants abandoned the land in droves to become industrial workers. Most of the food produced by the collectives was simply requisitioned by the state [8].

Some of the blame for the débâcle of the right must be pinned on Bukharin. Although an able economist, he never produced a convincing plan to counter the dreams of the super-industrialisers.

The very weakness of the party required the Politburo to show a united face to the public. The leadership could not afford to be seen engaging in infighting and factionalism. Controversies did burst into print, but Stalin's creeping control of the media dictated how the debate was conducted. The press gradually became a vehicle of the ruling faction, in which defeated political opponents were pilloried mercilessly without any right of reply. By 1929 all non-party journals had been closed down and there were no private publishing houses left.

Stalin also enjoyed his fair share of luck. Had Yakov Sverdlov not died in 1919 he would have been the natural candidate for the post of Secretary-General. Also Lenin's death saved Stalin from almost certain demotion. Dzerzhinsky, head of the political police – the *Cheka*,* renamed the OGPU (United State Political Administration) in 1922 – and on the left, died in July 1926. He had also been head of VSNKh, a key economic institution. His death opened the way to the appointment of Kuibyshev, an ally of Stalin and an advocate of forced industrialisation.

PART TWO: DESCRIPTIVE ANALYSIS

2 THE THIRTIES

POLITICS AND THE ECONOMY

After the war scare of 1927 [5] came the fear of foreign economic intervention. Wrecking was taking place in several industries and crises had occurred in others – or so Stalin claimed in April 1928. The following month he put the nation's youth on the alert: 'Comrades, our class enemies do exist. They not only exist but are growing and trying to act against Soviet power.' Then it was announced that a large-scale conspiracy involving engineers in the Shakhty areas of the Donbass had been uncovered. Stalin skilfully used the perceived threats to Soviet power to create an atmosphere of tension and apprehension. The coiled-up energy of the population could thereby be released and directed towards the achievement of specific targets. The first Five-Year Plan (FYP)* set these goals. In December 1929 it was decided that the plan could be achieved in four years and in the end it ran from 1 October 1928 to 31 December 1932. Plan goals were continually increased irrespective of economic rationality, as human will overruled mathematical calculations. As one planner stated: 'There are no fortresses which we Bolsheviks cannot storm'. The Great Depression, which began in 1929 in the advanced industrial states, added fuel to the conviction that the Bolsheviks were on the highway to success.

The Soviet leadership appears to have been surprised how easy it was to speed up collectivisation. Party officials in several selected areas competed with one another and when they proved successful Stalin and the key officials concerned with collectivisation, Molotov and Kaganovich, knew that they could outstrip the modest aim of collectivising 20 per cent of the sown area laid down for 1932 [69].

The number of peasants in collective farms of all types doubled between June and October 1929, and Stalin declared on 7 November 1929 that the great movement towards collectivisation was under way [8]. The Politburo stated on 5 January 1930 that large-scale *kulak* production was to be replaced by large-scale *kolkhoz* production. Ominously, for the better-off farmers it also proclaimed the 'liquidation of the *kulaks* as a class'.

It was hoped that the collectivisation of the key grain-growing areas, the North Caucasus and the Volga region, would be completed by the spring of 1931 at the latest and the other grain-growing areas by the spring of 1932. A vital role in rapid collectivisation was played by the 25,000 workers who descended on the countryside to aid the 'voluntary' process. The 'twenty-five thousanders', as they were called, brooked no opposition. They were all vying with one another for the approbation of the party. Officially, force was only permissible against *kulaks*, but the middle and poor peasants were soon sucked into the maelstrom of violence. *Kulaks* were expelled from their holdings and their stock and implements handed over to the *kolkhoz*. What was to become of them? Stalin was brutally frank: 'It is ridiculous and foolish to talk at length about dekulakisation. ... When the head is off, one does not grieve for the hair. There is another question no less ridiculous: whether *kulaks* should be allowed to join the collective farms? Of course not, for they are the sworn enemies of the collective farm movement.' *Kulaks* were divided into three classes. The first consisted of about 63,000 'counter-revolutionary' families who were to be executed or exiled and have their property confiscated. Group two was made up of 150,000 households labelled 'exploiters' or 'active opponents' of collectivisation. These were to be deported to the remote regions of the east and north, but permitted to retain some possessions. Another group was composed of between 396,000 and 852,000 households who were to be allowed to remain in their home region but on land outside the collectives. (This meant, in fact, on land which was at that time not arable.) If one assumes a modest five members per household, the first two groups amounted to over one million persons. No one in the Politburo cared whether they survived or not. Others abandoned their home villages and made for the towns, desperately trying to beg enough for survival. *Kulak* children were sometimes left to die, since their deported fathers belonged to the 'wrong class'.

Sufficient sporadic peasant violence met the 'twenty-five thousanders' and their cohorts to make the leadership nervous. Thereupon Stalin changed course and launched an attack on all those officials who had herded peasants into collectives against their will. His article in *Pravda* on 2 March 1930 was entitled 'Dizzy with Success' [*Doc. 3*]. In it he pilloried the wayward officials, but this was mere double-talk. It was he, in fact, who had driven them on! *Pravda* became a best-seller in the countryside as desperate officials attempted to restrict circulation. There was a stampede to leave the *kolkhozes*, and only 23 per cent of the peasants were left in collective farms by 1 June 1930. Stalin had not lost his nerve; he merely wished to ensure that the spring sowing was completed. Afterwards the collectivisation offensive was resumed, and the beaten peasants took to slaughtering their livestock and breaking their implements rather than see them collectivised. Mikhail Sholokhov, the Nobel Prize-winning Soviet novelist, catches the atmosphere in *Virgin Soil Upturned*. ' "Slaughter! You won't get meat in the *kolkhoz*", crept the insidious rumours. And they slaughtered. They ate until they could eat no more. Young and old suffered from indigestion. At dinner time tables groaned under boiled or roast meat. Everyone had a greasy mouth, everyone hiccoughed as if at a wake. Everyone blinked like an owl, as if inebriated from eating' [5 *p. 162*].

Livestock numbers in 1932 were less than half those of 1928. To the government the tractor was the symbol of the mechanisation and modernisation of agriculture and the trump card of the new *kolkhozes* and state farms, *sovkhozes* [8]. It penetrated the countryside more rapidly than expected. Since so many draught animals had been slaughtered, scarce resources had to be diverted to the production of even more tractors. The shortage of cattle and sheep meant less leather and wool for consumer goods.

Timid voices were raised about the breakneck speed of industrialisation. Could the pace not be slowed down a little? Stalin firmly rejected such thinking [*Doc. 4*]. He even wanted the economy to expand more rapidly, on the grounds that with imperialist vultures circling overhead the Soviet Union had to become strong enough to keep them at bay. 'Specialist baiting' was a popular sport during the early years of the first FYP [8]. After the Shakhty trial in 1928 came the 'industrial party' trial in November–December 1930, when industrial experts confessed to wrecking and other heinous crimes. The Shakhty trial was followed by the arrest of thousands of 'bourgeois' or non-party engineers. By 1931 half of the engineers and technical workers in the Donbass, a key industrial region, had been arrested [108]. What did the charge of wrecking amount to? If a machine broke down – as happened quite often, due to the fact that the peasant turned worker had to learn on the job – someone higher up was to blame. If imported machinery [5] was not adequately used it could be construed as wrecking. It may seem paradoxical that at a time when their skills were desperately needed, 'bourgeois' and foreign engineers were being held behind bars. However, there was a rationale behind the arrests: the leadership was desperately anxious to break down all resistance to central directives. The 'bourgeois' engineer could see the the orders were not feasible and said so. Moscow wanted engineers who would attempt to do the impossible.

A declared opponent of the campaign against 'bourgeois' engineers was Sergo Ordzhonikidze, who became head of the Supreme Council of the National Economy (VSNKh) at the end of 1930 and thereby the *de facto* leader of the drive for industrialisation. He appears to have influenced Stalin's decision to call a halt to the campaign. On 23 June 1931 the Secretary-General declared that the policy of considering every specialist an 'undetected criminal and wrecker' should be dropped [*Doc. 5*]. Show trials of engineers did not completely cease, however, as the case against the Metro-Vickers engineers in 1933 demonstrated.

The change of heart towards the experts was accompanied by a dramatic change in the fortunes of labour. The years 1928–31 saw workers exercise an influence over production never again to be equalled. Shock workers and shock brigades showed the workers the way, and there was a great deal of worker initiative as hierarchy was played down. This happened at a time when the planners could not accurately plot the way ahead. Some members of the leadership, working on the assumption that socialism meant a moneyless economy, believed that the exchange of products would replace money as NEP was phased out. Indeed, many of them in 1930 thought that this stage was fast approaching. It was also widely assumed that society could be transformed very rapidly and that workers would be motivated by enthusiasm, so that an end could be made to payment by result. In July 1931, however, Stalin changed his approach. He attacked the prevalent egalitarianism and proposed wage differentials which reflected skill and responsibility [*Doc. 6*]. The ideas of the American time and motion expert, F.W. Taylor, found favour, and engineers were given the task of setting scientifically based norms. Authority was reinvested in specialists and engineers.

The first FYP was a period of genuine enthusiasm, and prodigious achievements were recorded in production. The 'impossible' targets galvanised people into action, and more was achieved than would have been the case had orthodox advice been followed. New cities, such as Magnitogorsk in the Urals, rose from the ground. According to official statistics the first FYP in industry was fulfilled [*Doc. 7*, no. 5] with the plan for producers' goods – the production of the means of production (heavy industry) – being over-fulfilled [no. 9]. Consumption goods (light industry), on the other hand, fell short of the target [no. 10]. These figures are open to criticism, however. They are expressed in 1926–27 prices, but many of the goods produced during the plan were not made in 1926–27. Money values in roubles were used instead, and these certainly erred on the high side. Various western economists have recomputed the results and their estimates range from 59.7 to 69.9 per cent fulfilment [nos. 6–8].

Whatever the figures, a great engineering industry was in the making and the rise in the output of machinery, machine tools, turbines and tractors was very impressive. Ukraine, the Volga, the Urals and the Kuzbass (south-west Siberia) saw most expansion. Engineering enterprises in the Leningrad and Moscow regions were modernised and expanded. Industry also penetrated the less well developed republics, especially Kazakhstan and Central Asia. Power for expanding Ukrainian industry flowed from the huge Dnieper dam which was completed during these years. The plan for railway expansion was less than half achieved but canals increased rapidly, often using forced labour, as in the case of the Volga–White Sea canal [8].

Not surprisingly, the agricultural performance was abysmal [*Doc.* 7, no. 11]. The rush out of the countryside led to the over-fulfilment of the labour plan [no. 16] and unemployment in the cities had disappeared by 1932. Industry took on many more workers than planned [no. 17]. All this meant that money wages were far in excess of the plan [no. 18]. Thus there was even more money than expected chasing the few consumer goods on offer. Living standards were miserably low, and if they were low in the towns they were even worse in the countryside.

Despite the over-fulfilment of the labour plan, industrial production was officially only a fraction over the plan [no. 5]. This meant that labour productivity was very low, and came as a great disappointment to the planners. Determined efforts were made to increase labour discipline during the FYP. The first legislation involving prison sentences for those who violated labour discipline was passed in January 1931. Work books were introduced for all industrial and transport workers in February 1931, and the death sentence could be applied for the theft of state or collective farm property as from August 1932. Missing a day's work could mean instant dismissal after November 1932, and the internal passport

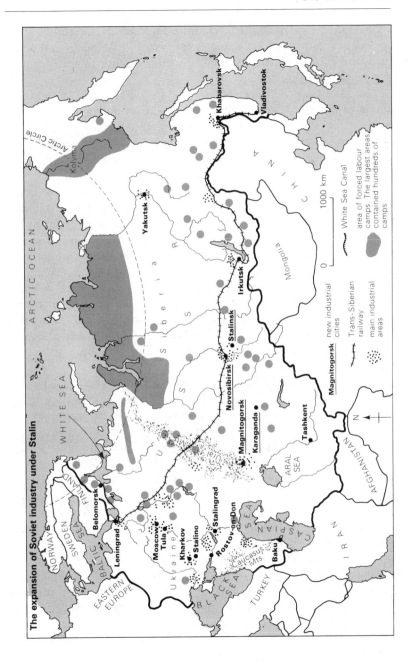

The expansion of Soviet industry under Stalin

Magnitogorsk new industrial cities

Trans-Siberian railway

main industrial areas

White Sea Canal

area of forced labour camps. The largest areas contained hundreds of camps

1000 km

ARCTIC OCEAN

Arctic Circle

Kolyma

Khabarovsk

Vladivostok

CHINA

Yakutsk

Mongolia

Irkutsk

Stalinsk

Novosibirsk

Magnitogorsk

Karaganda

Tashkent

AFGHANISTAN

WHITE SEA

Belomorsk

Leningrad

Moscow

Tula

Kharkov

Stalino

Stalingrad

Rostov-on-Don

Baku

ARAL SEA

CASPIAN SEA

Caucasus Mts

BLACK SEA

TURKEY

IRAN

NORWAY

SWEDEN

FINLAND

BALTIC SEA

EASTERN EUROPE

Ukraine

Siberia

U S S R

Ural

(not issued to *kolkhozniks*)* was introduced on 27 December 1932 to restrict movement and increase control [8]. Such draconian measures bear eloquent testimony to the difficulty of transforming the peasant into a worker.

The industrial achievements of the first FYP were mainly the result of utilising the available capacity more fully, including the extra plant which came on stream as a consequence of pre-1928 investment. Plant started during the first FYP was completed, in the main, in 1934–36, and the investment plan was only half fulfilled (*Doc. 7*, no. 26].

However, not everyone was willing to put up with low living standards indefinitely. Stalin, speaking at a CC plenum in January 1933, had a message for all the grumblers: 'We have without doubt achieved a situation in which the material conditions of workers and peasants are improving year by year. The only people who doubt this are the sworn enemies of Soviet power.'

The mayhem of collectivisation and low yields of 1932 led to a famine in 1933. It was made even worse by the need to seize seed grain from the farms to build up stocks to feed the Red Army if a conflict with Japan occurred in the Far East. The number of deaths from starvation was 7.2–8.1 million [123] but these were not mentioned in the Soviet press.

Thus the second FYP (1933–37) got off to a very inauspicious start and the XVIIth Party Congress in January–February 1934 redrafted it. The new version revealed that Soviet planning had become more realistic, for this time the targets set did not belong to cloud cuckoo land. Agriculture was in a parlous state in 1933 but improved rapidly afterwards. Although there were still about nine million peasants outside the collective farm sector in 1934, by 1937 they had practically all been collectivised. High taxes and compulsory deliveries were levied on the peasant, and when he could not meet his obligations all his goods and belongings were sold to meet the deficit.

Livestock numbers recovered rapidly after the depredations of the early 1930s [8]. This was due in large part to the state's willingness to permit farmers to own their own animals – within strict limits, of course. Each household was also allowed a private plot. Surplus produce could be sold legally in towns in the *kolkhoz* market, though only by the producers themselves. No middlemen were permitted to reappear.

A Congress was convened in 1935 to draft a model charter for the *kolkhozes*, which was to stay on the statute book until the early

1970s. The *kolkhoz* was defined as a voluntary cooperative working land provided by the state rent-free in perpetuity. The chairman was to be elected by the members, but in practice the *kolkhoz* enjoyed little autonomy since its goals were set by the party and the government. The mechanical work was done under contract by machine tractor stations [8]. Thus the available machinery was spread around as much as possible. The farms paid for such services in kind. Unlike state farms or *sovkhozes*, collective farms did not offer their members a guaranteed wage before 1966. If the farm did well, the profits were shared out at the end of the year. If results were poor, little or nothing was paid out. Hence it was possible for a *kolkhoznik* to work assiduously and to receive little or no reward for his labours. Not surprisingly he quickly came to realise that the private plot was his staff of life and that his cow was especially valuable [*Doc. 26*]. He therefore devoted his energies to his private plot and merely went through the motions on the collective farm. The girls often opted out of agriculture altogether by moving to the towns, and the more ambitious young men followed them.

The second FYP was over-fulfilled, in general, by 3 per cent [*Doc. 7, no. 5*]. The engineering industry again expanded rapidly. The output of steel almost trebled, the main reason for this being that the great plants begun during the first FYP entered production. Magnitogorsk, Kuznetsk and Zaporozhe, for example, became great industrial centres. Karaganda (Kazakhstan), the Kuzbass and the Urals saw a great expansion of coal production; the generation of electricity grew but oil output was disappointing as Baku and the Urals–Volga fields failed to cope with their technical problems. Industry was spread around the country, even to the non-Slav republics where the return on investment was lower that in 'older' industrial areas [8].

The pious hopes about according consumer goods greater emphasis bore no fruit [no. 10]. One of the reasons for this was the increasing share of industrial production being devoted to defence – officially only 3.4 per cent of total budget expenditure in 1933 but 16.5 per cent in 1937. (Real defence expenditure in 1933 appears to have been about 12 per cent.) Agriculture flopped again [no. 11]; indeed no FYP for agriculture ever achieved its targets in the Soviet Union.

The number of workers in the economy as a whole, and especially in industry, fell below the levels projected by the FYP [no. 16], but as output had exceeded the targets this meant that labour productivity was rising faster than expected. One of the contributory factors to this was the impact of the Stakhanovite movement, named after Aleksei Stakhanov, who on 30–31 August 1935 had shown just what *could* be done by mining 102 tonnes of coal in five hours and forty-five minutes (the equivalent of fourteen norms). Doing the work of fourteen men is an astonishing feat, but Stakhanov's achievement was also eloquent testimony to the low productivity of Soviet miners. Needless to say Stakhanov did not achieve the feat on his own: he had all the help he needed and all the machinery was in working order.

Real wages increased greatly during the second FYP but were still lower in 1937 than in 1928 and in that year were little better than in 1913. Rationing was gradually phased out in 1935, but even with a ration card (only issued to workers and employees) there was no guarantee that the desired goods would be available. Free market prices were very high, reflecting especially the shortage of bread, a staple food [8].

The third FYP (1938–41) was adopted at the XVIIIth Party Congress in 1939, but was cut short after three and a half years by the German invasion [105]. It reaffirmed the emphasis placed on heavy industry, but it also increased defence expenditure to 18 per cent of GDP in 1940. As a consequence the living standards of workers and employees stagnated and may even have fallen slightly by 1941.

Forced labour, supervised by the People's Commissariat of Internal Affairs (NKVD),* made a significant contribution to the fulfilment of the plan. Western estimates of the number of prisoners in 1941 range from 3.5 million to 15 million. Recent Soviet research has produced a figure of 1.9 million in 1941 rising to 2.5 million in 1952 [110]. It would appear that the Soviet figures only include part of those doing compulsory labour.

Government attitudes towards the workers became noticeably harsher in 1939 and 1940. Hitherto workers had been able to choose their place of work, and this produced a high labour turnover as they sought to improve their lot. In 1940, however, the state decreed that the free labour market was to end. No worker could change his job without permission, and skilled workers and specialists could be directed anywhere. Absenteeism, which could mean being twenty minutes late for work, became a criminal offence and one woman was actually convicted of the crime while she was in a maternity ward. The legislation stayed on the statute book until 1956, and if judges were soft on offenders they were put in the dock themselves. Theft was severely dealt with. One man who worked in a flour mill brought home a handful of grain for his hungry family, and was sentenced to five years' imprisonment. Social benefits for most workers were cut and fees were introduced for students in institutions of higher learning and for senior pupils in secondary schools. The population must have been frightened.

CULTURE

Education changed dramatically as the entire pedagogical system was transformed. Schools were handed over to collective farms or enterprises, pupils and teachers abandoned formal learning and sought to learn through 'productive labour' or were mobilised to fulfil the plan. There was even talk of the 'withering away of the school' altogether. Universities were transferred to Vesenkha (VSNKh) or the major economic commissariats. The majority were restructured along functional lines, involving narrow specialisms. 'Bourgeois' academics were, like school teachers, hounded out. However, by 1932 literacy was back in fashion. The socialist substitute, the *rabfak*, had produced high drop-out rates and little technical expertise. (One of those who dropped out was Nikita Khrushchev.) Selection reappeared and by the end of 1936 non-proletarians could again enter higher education. Russian nationalism was promoted and all other nations were referred to as 'younger brothers'. Tuition fees had to be paid for the final three forms of secondary education. Compulsory uniforms were introduced (including pigtails for girls) and these remained until the end of the Soviet era. Out of experimentation developed a fine educational system with a particularly good record in the pure sciences.

The party did not attempt to control all aspects of culture during the 1920s, and a 1925 decree made this clear [5]. The defeat of the right, however, had serious repercussions, since several key writers were linked to Bukharin. The All-Russian Association of Proletarian Writers (RAPP)* was in the ascendant in 1928 and propagated the hegemony of working-class values in fiction. There was only one fly in the ointment as far as RAPP was concerned, namely the All-Russian Union of Writers (AUW).* The latter tried to keep politics out of their fiction but although RAPP disapproved strongly of this attitude, most of the leading Russian writers were members of the AUW. Undeterred, RAPP launched a campaign against Evgeny Zamyatin, the AUW chairman, and Boris Pilnyak, head of the Leningrad branch, accusing them of publishing anti-Soviet works abroad. They were found guilty, and the AUW was dissolved and replaced by the All-Russian Union of Soviet Writers (AUSW).* About half of the former AUW members were denied admission to the new organisation, and since they could not legally publish unless they were members, they faced a stark choice: recant and seek admission, or give up hope of publishing in the Soviet Union. RAPP was jubilant. However, in 1930 Stalin wrote an article for the party journal *Bolshevik*, in which he argued that nothing should be published which was contrary to the official point of view. This should have warned RAPP (which believed that literature should tell the truth, warts and all) that party goals might not always be identical with its own. In fact, the party disbanded both RAPP and AUSW in 1932 and set up a single organisation, the Union of Soviet Writers.

The end of RAPP was the end of an era in Russian literature. Writing during the years 1928–31 saw the glorification of the small man, as everyone pulled together to build the new USSR [125]. Plots displayed an absence of hierarchy and experts and managers faded into the background. The machine was worshipped; indeed only a country as backward as the Soviet Union could have placed so much faith in technology as the answer to man's problems. The rest of Europe had had the myth of the good machine exploded during the First World War, but for post-war Russia, noise was still a sign of progress, and the smoke belching out of factory chimneys a symbol of a brighter future.

After 1931 the literary hero changes. The manager, the expert, the party official, in other words the decision-makers, take over. The writer had also to be a skilled craftsman, the 'engineer of the soul', as Stalin graphically put it. His frame of reference was laid down by Andrei Zhdanov in April 1934 at the 1st Congress of the Union of Soviet Writers. Socialist realism was to be the guiding light [5]. In essence it meant building the brave new world with the bricks of the present. Literature was to uplift the reader so that he would become a more efficient constructor of socialism. It was to be deliberately didactic, and optimism was compulsory. Every novel, like a Hollywood picture of the period, had to have a happy ending as the hero or heroine battled against impossible odds to final victory.

The main hero, of course, was Stalin. Another was the Russian nation and its great figures; Peter the Great and Ivan the Terrible walked again. This tide of nationalism boded ill for the other nationalities. Stalin formulated the slogan 'National in form, Socialist in content', to describe what was permissible. In reality this amounted to little more than saying, for example, in Uzbek, what was being said about Stalin and Russia in Russian. The national heroes who had fought against imperial Russian control were banished; the local bards were swept aside and replaced by Russian luminaries. The purges which wiped out the non-Russian élites completed the process.

THE PURGES

All the show trials between 1928 and 1934 linked the accused to the economy [108]: the Shakhty engineers, the 'industrial party' trial, the Menshevik trial of 1931, the two secret trials of March 1933 which resulted in seventy state farm and People's Commissariat of Agriculture officials being shot, and the trial of the Metro-Vickers engineers. Other trials led to the passing of the death sentence on food scientists and bacteriologists. The trials all had to be carefully prepared since they had to appear plausible both inside the Soviet Union and outside. The paraphernalia of the great Purge Trials of 1936–38 was already in place: the written confessions, often to the most preposterous crimes, the bullying, sarcastic behaviour of the prosecutor, and the complete absence of any rules of evidence [108]. All the shortcomings of the economy were to be blamed on the unfortunates in the dock.

The only major trial with political overtones which occurred before 1934 was that involving a group around a communist called M.N. Ryutin. They had produced a 200-page indictment of Stalin and his regime from a Bukharinist point of view in late summer 1932, in which the Secretary-General was described as the 'evil genius of the Russian revolution who, motivated by personal desire for power and revenge, had brought the revolution to the brink of destruction'. Since they wanted Stalin removed, he took this to mean that they were going to kill him, and therefore demanded the death penalty. But a majority of the Politburo was opposed to such an extreme measure, and in the event Ryutin and his followers were merely expelled from the party. Since many other party members had seen the offending document and had not reported it, the opportunity was seized to purge the whole organisation. Some 800,000 members were expelled in 1933 and a further 340,000 in 1934. The Ryutin affair rankled with Stalin, and time and again during the Purge Trials reference was made to it.

Stalin was shaken by the suicide of his second wife, Nadezhda Alliluyeva, in November 1932. She took her own life as a protest against the brutalities of collectivisation. Stalin never remarried and over time isolated himself more and more from his family. He seems to have lived surrounded by men, and although Khrushchev records that on one occasion he encountered a 'dark Caucasian beauty' in the Kremlin, she scurried away in an instant.

The murder of Sergei Kirov, party secretary in Leningrad, on 1 December 1934 set in motion a train of events which resulted in death for hundreds of thousands of people. Some of the details of the assassination are still not known, but it would appear that Stalin himself was implicated. Kirov was the only credible political alternative to Stalin, for he had been elected a secretary at the XVIIth Party Congress in 1934 at which Stalin had lost his post of Secretary-General. Kirov had been approached by delegates to stand for the post of Secretary-General but declined and reported this to Stalin. It is tempting to regard this episode as sealing Kirov's fate. With Kirov dead, much repressive legislation was introduced. One of the chief targets was the party itself, as inhibitions about spilling Bolshevik blood were cast aside. The XVIIth Congress, described at the time as the 'Congress of Victors', might more appropriately have been called the 'Congress of the Condemned', for 1,108 of its 1,966 delegates were executed and 98 of the 139 members of the CC elected at the Congress were shot in the years following.

The punitive legislation introduced – which included, for example, the death penalty for boys of twelve – was consonant with Stalin's views of the class struggle. Classes would disappear, he said, 'not as a result of the slackening of class conflict but as a result of its intensification'. The state would wither away 'not through the weakening of its power but through it becoming as strong as possible so as to defeat the remnants of the dying classes and to defend itself against capitalist encirclement'. This really was standing Marx on his head and is another example of Stalin's ideological relativism. An orthodox Marxist would expect classes to disappear as class conflict declines and for the state to wither away as the need for it disappears. Marx saw the state as an oppressive instrument used by the minority to oppress the majority.

Paradoxically, at the same time as these punitive measures were being applied, the Stalin constitution of 1936 – the 'most democratic in the world', as Stalin described it – came into effect. This introduced a bicameral legislature, the Soviet of the Union and the Soviet of Nationalities, collectively known as the USSR Supreme Soviet.* The role of the local soviets now changed. Hitherto they had been seen as both legislative and executive organs, not mere extensions of the central authority, constituting a unified system of equal links of varying sizes. They had also been seen as peculiar to the stage of the dictatorship of the proletariat. The 1936 constitution shattered the unity of the soviets. Local soviets (all those below republican level) were reduced to the status of local authorities. The Supreme Soviets ('the supreme organs of the soviets') became legislative organs; and the government ('the supreme organ of state power') became the executive organ. The Supreme Soviets even began to call themselves parliaments, despite Lenin's contempt for that institution.

The new constitution stated that the foundations of socialism had been laid and that the exploiting classes had ceased to exist. There were now only fraternal classes – the working class and the collective farm peasantry – and they coexisted harmoniously with the intelligentsia, defined as a stratum rather than a class since it owned no property.

Freedom of speech, of the press, of assembly and of religious observance were guaranteed by the 1936 constitution. However, it was pointed out that the party remained the key institution and it was clear to every Soviet citizen that the party's interests would override any personal or group interest. Nevertheless, the Soviet Union appeared to be moving in the right direction and made a refreshing contrast to the rest of Europe where fascism was on the march.

There were three great Show Trials during the years 1936–38 [108]. The first took place in August 1936 and involved Kamenev and Zinoviev, along with sundry minor officials. Trotsky was introduced as the arch villain and it was claimed that he had ordered numerous assassinations and wreckings. Andrei Vyshinsky, who became notorious as a brutal prosecutor, demanded in his closing speech that these mad dogs be shot, every last one of them! They were all shot, but it was Stalin who was the real judge. Vyshinsky epitomised a certain type of official who slavishly served Stalin. As an ex-Menshevik he felt that he had repeatedly to reaffirm his credentials of loyalty to the regime.

The second great Show Trial should have involved Bukharin, Rykov and Tomsky in September 1936, but it was cancelled. Tomsky cheated the executioner by taking his own life and it was possible that neither Bukharin nor Rykov would make the obligatory confession. Also Yagoda, the man in charge, lost his position to Nikolai Ezhov in September 1936. Yagoda's dismissal may have been connected with his failure to deliver Bukharin and

Rykov to the executioner. Everyone who knew Ezhov before he became head of the NKVD commented on how nice a man he was. There was, however, nothing nice about his two years in office (he was replaced by Lavrenty Beria in December 1938). They were the most dreadful peacetime years in the history of the Soviet Union. During the *Ezhovshchina*, the Ezhov times, blood flowed in rivers, and the guilt or innocence of the accused was completely immaterial. The political police had their plan targets like everyone else and were certainly not going to underfulfil them. According to a report, dated 11 December 1953, sent to Khrushchev and Malenkov, the total number condemned by the political police (*Cheka*, NKVD, etc.) between 1921 and 1953 was 4,060,306. The number shot was 799,455 of which no less than 681,692 were executed during 1937 and 1938, the *Ezhovshchina*. Lesser peaks of repression were 1930–33, 1942 and 1945–46. Another remarkable statistic is that over the years 1923–53, in the RSFSR alone, 39.1 million persons were sentenced by the regular courts (excluding the special NKVD courts, special councils and tribunals). If one excludes those under the age of 14 and over 60 years old, then during the course of one generation, from 1923 to 1953, every third citizen was sentenced for non-political offences. In comparison, the highest number in prison in the immediate pre-war period was 111,800 in 1912.

The second great Show Trial turned out to involve Pyatakov, mentioned by Lenin in his 'Testament': Sokolnikov, a signatory of the Brest-Litovsk treaty and later a Commissar for Finance who had resisted the wild targets of the first FYP; and various other party functionaries. They were all lumped together as an 'Anti-Soviet Trotskyist Centre' [1]. Pyatakov debased himself but nevertheless was shot. Sokolnikov died in a labour camp in 1939.

The turn of the military came in due course. Marshal Tukhachevsky, a deputy Commissar for Defence and a leading strategic thinker, and many other top military figures were branded as traitors and shot in June 1937. Then followed a veritable slaughter of the top brass. All eleven deputy Commissars of Defence and seventy-five of the eighty members of the Supreme Military Council were executed. All eight admirals were shot. In total 35,000, half of the officer corps, were either executed or imprisoned. As Khrushchev was to admit later, it had all been a ghastly mistake since the charges against the officers were baseless [12].

The last great Show Trial opened on 2 March 1938 and involved the pair who had previously slipped the net, Bukharin and Rykov.

Others thrown in included Yagoda, getting a taste of his own medicine. Vyshinsky branded them as the 'Bloc of the right wingers and Trotskyites', and the inevitable death sentence followed.

Foreign communists in exile in the Soviet Union were mown down like ripe corn, the NKVD being especially severe on the Germans and Poles. The greatest prize of all, however, eluded them until 21 August 1940, when an agent put an ice pick through Trotsky's skull in Mexico [5].

After such a catalogue of methodical madness the question must arise: was Stalin himself a victim of the frenzy of the period? Did he lose his sanity for a while? Svetlana Alliluyeva, his daughter, believes that officials such as Beria poisoned his mind and convinced him that the mad accusations were true [15; 50]. This is not so. Stalin himself edited the indictment against Pyatakov, Sokolnikov, Radek and others for the second great Show Trial. All lists of condemned were forwarded to Stalin and during 1938 at least 383 lists, containing 44,000 names of whom 39,000 were executed, were passed on to him. Stalin signed 362 lists, Molotov 373, Voroshilov 195, Kaganovich 191 and Zhdanov 177. Stalin's Politburo colleagues were enthusiastic in their support of these repressions. They often wrote comments in the margin encouraging the NKVD to step up the torture: for example, against certain names: 'beat again and again!' [109] [*Doc. 13*]. The terror was turned off like a tap in 1939, but the show trials had had a momentum of their own. The NKVD did not have to go and look for suspects; they were inundated with denunciations [*Doc. 14*]. Such was the spirit of the times that in order to avoid being denounced one had to denounce everyone else first. There were even targets set for the number of people one had to denounce in a given period.

An understanding of the period can be gleaned from the fortunes of two persons caught up in the NKVD net, Osip and Nadezhda Mandelstam [38]. Thousands, perhaps millions, had similar experiences.

Osip Mandelstam was a gifted poet but never became a Bolshevik. Like many other writers his patron was Bukharin. He was arrested in May 1934 for composing a poem which contained an unflattering reference to Stalin [*Doc. 8*]: 'All we hear is the Kremlin mountaineer/The murderer and peasant slayer.' His wife Nadezhda recalls the techniques used to force confessions [*Doc. 9*]: lack of sleep, bright lights shining in the eyes, poor food, the deliberate telling of lies to confuse the prisoner and make him more anxious – 'such and such a person had been arrested and had confessed everything' – and physical beatings, although Mandelstam was spared these. This goes a long way towards explaining why innocent men and women confessed to the most outlandish crimes. Broken down they were willing to admit anything providing they could just get some sleep and be left in peace. Of course some did not break down: they were the prisoners who never appeared at the trials. Nadezhda Mandelstam draws a distinction between the type of person who was an interrogator before 1937 and afterwards. Until 1937 the Chekist or NKVD man was often well read in Russian literature, the sort of person who would have been all in favour of RAPP and delighted to display his culture, convinced that his work was helping to build the new Russia. In 1937 a new type took over; men who had little culture and no beliefs, and were only concerned with meeting their quota of confessions. Osip Mandelstam's interrogator, like many of the pre-1937 men, himself became a victim of the purges and was shot.

Denunciations flowed into the NKVD in torrents. Before 1937 they had to have a semblance of truth to be effective; afterwards it did not matter. Denunciations became a convenient way of acquiring something desirable. If one's superior was found guilty, promotion was in prospect. If neighbours were removed, a flat would become vacant. Personal relations became hazardous, for anyone might let something slip which would then be reported to the police. Spontaneous and personal openness became things of the past. Parents could never be completely frank at home, since something they said might be repeated at school with disastrous consequences. If the head of the household was sentenced the whole family fell into disgrace. Wives and children could then be expelled from the cities and obliged to live at least 105 km away. Life for the convicted was relatively easy before 1937 [*Doc. 10*], but then things got worse. Wives were interned in camps and small children were confined in special institutions [*Doc. 11*].

Mandelstam was saved from death by the intervention of Bukharin. He was packed off to the Urals, but a further plea resulted in him and his wife being allowed to reside in Voronezh. They spent three years in exile in Voronezh and returned to Moscow in May 1937. Mandelstam had even tried to write an Ode to Stalin in January 1937 in order to rehabilitate himself and his wife but the words would not come. He and his wife were again thrown out of Moscow in June 1937 and told to reside at least 105 km from the capital, since they were 'convicted persons'. They eventually moved to Kalinin, north-west of Moscow. Mandelstam travelled frequently to Moscow and begged the Union of Soviet Writers for work. He and his wife were given accommodation in a rest home east of Moscow, but shortly after their arrival, on 1 May 1938, Mandelstam was arrested and was never seen again. His wife returned to Kalinin and narrowly escaped arrest. She then moved to a small town north-east of Moscow, coming in regularly to the capital in search of information about her husband. She eventually discovered that he had died in a labour camp, probably in December 1938.

FOREIGN POLICY

The rise of fascism was completely misinterpreted in Moscow, where it was assumed to be the most predatory face of finance capital, with only a limited capacity to endure, if it ever came to power. The Comintern, the Russian Communist Party wearing its foreign suit, came to the conclusion that the German National Socialists (NSDAP)* were claiming to do the impossible. They promised to put German industry back on its feet, which implied that big business would do very well, but at the same time they canvassed the votes of small businessmen, shopkeepers and farmers. They promised the latter they would protect them against unfair competition and secure a bright future for them, yet in order to do this the Nazis would have to restrict the activities of the industrial giants. In other words the Nazis could not satisfy both sides. The Italian fascists were not seen as a threat to the Soviet Union, so why should German fascism be different? The Social Democrats (SPD)* were regarded as the main enemy and labelled 'social fascists'. In Germany the SPD was the main supporter of the Weimar republic, and it was assumed in Moscow that the destruction of the SPD would topple the republic.

The breath-taking ease with which Hitler and the NSDAP swept the Communist Party of Germany (KPD)* off the political stage, the pusillanimity of the other political parties and the Führer's ruthlessness in disposing of Ernst Röhm and the SA (*Sturmabteilung* or storm troops) as part of a deal with the German army, the *Reichswehr*, rudely awakened Moscow. The Comintern, at its VIIth and final Congress in August 1935, called for the formation of a popular front. Western governments were slow to react. After all, the previous Comintern policy had been to appeal to rank-and-file social democrats over the heads of their leaders, who were publicly vilified.

The Soviet Union set out to repair her fences with the rest of Europe. She joined the League of Nations in 1934 and signed a treaty with France in 1935 which was extended to embrace Czechoslovakia [5]. The 1936 constitution, partly for external consumption, made the USSR more attractive. However, 1936 was a bad year for Moscow. The German remilitarisation of the Rhineland, the signing of the Anti-Comintern Pact by Germany, Italy and Japan, and the onset of the Spanish Civil War, with the Soviet Union as the main ally of the Spanish republic, boded ill for Soviet hopes.

The Munich Agreement of September 1938, from which the Soviet Union was excluded, led Stalin to doubt whether France and Great Britain would ever stand up to Germany.

Stalin had at least two alternatives so far as policy towards Germany was concerned. He could enter into an alliance with France and Great Britain and thereby effectively checkmate the Third Reich, which could not face a war on two fronts. However, the Soviet leader could not be absolutely sure that France and Great Britain would remain committed if war with Germany did break out. Stalin's other option was to sign a pact with Hitler and unleash the dogs of war westwards. When he came to the conclusion that war was inevitable his main objective was to keep the USSR out of the conflict. After what he had done to the Red Army and Navy this was the most prudent course. The Soviet Union began negotiating seriously in May 1939, when Litvinov, a Jew, was replaced as Commissar for Foreign Affairs by Molotov. The German–Soviet Non-Aggression Pact was signed by Ribbentrop and Molotov in Moscow on 23 August 1939 (Stalin and Hitler never met) and it was consequently only a matter of time before Hitler attacked in the west. Moscow was alarmed by the rapid success of the German *Blitzkrieg* in Poland and by the fact that neither France nor Great Britain made any move to attack Germany. Stalin even began to fear that the *Wehrmacht* (German armed forces) would not stop at the agreed demarcation line in Poland and would carry on to invade the Soviet Union. He therefore ordered the Red Army to enter Poland in September 1939 to secure the USSR's slice of the bargain. France and Great Britain obligingly did not treat this as an act of war against them.

With Finland part of her zone of influence, Moscow pressed the Finns to accept a frontier away from Leningrad. The Soviets also wanted naval bases on Finnish soil, but Helsinki would not countenance this. The Red Army therefore launched an assault against Finland on 30 November 1939, but the Winter War highlighted its deficiencies, and led to the death of some 200,000 of its soldiers [5]. In order to forestall intervention by France and Great Britain, a lenient peace was signed in March 1940. Great efforts were made afterwards to improve the fighting capacity of the Red Army.

Hitler regarded a war between Germany and the Soviet Union as inevitable. The world was too small for two such ambitious ideologies as fascism and communism. Stalin considered that a conflict could be avoided. He thought that Hitler could be bought off with concessions and believed that Germany had to defeat Great Britain first. This would give the Soviet Union the breathing space necessary to build up her armed might to such a pitch that the *Wehrmacht* would not invade.

Stalin handled his relations with Hitler very badly. Since the USSR was the weaker power he had to appease the German dictator. When Molotov visited Berlin in November 1940 Hitler proposed that the Soviet Union should joint the Tripartite Pact which linked Germany, Italy and Japan with Berlin's east European satellites. The bait was Soviet gains in the Black Sea area and in Central Asia. Molotov astonishingly then produced his own shopping list. Finland and southern Bukovina (Romania) were to fall under Soviet sway; Bulgaria was to form part of a Soviet security zone, as was Sweden; and notice was served that the Soviets had future designs on Hungary, Yugoslavia, Greece and even on part of German-occupied Poland. The Soviets also wanted military bases in the Dardanelles and a Soviet–Danish condominium over the Baltic. Shortly afterwards Stalin accepted the invitation to join the Tripartite Pact and demanded that the Soviet Union be permitted to expand through Iran to the Persian Gulf. Since the USSR militarily was in no position to make such demands on Germany, the only result of this démarche was to annoy Hitler and to fuel his doubts about the reliability of his new partner.

Stalin's demands revealed the weakness of the Soviet Union, and instead of pacifying Hitler they provoked him. Just why did Stalin act so clumsily? Perhaps he thought that if he did not make any demands Hitler would have regarded the Soviet Union as weak and afraid to assert its interests. Stalin remained unaware of his blunder, however, and the German invasion of 22 June 1941 took him completely by surprise, even though he had been forewarned by his own intelligence services. He simply refused to believe the information. The *Wehrmacht* had intended to attack earlier, in May

1941, but had been detained in Greece and Yugoslavia. Stalin thought he was safe in June, since this would be too late for a summer offensive.

If the prime goal of Soviet foreign policy during the 1930s was to keep the country out of a European war, then it was a dismal failure. The rise of fascism was looked on with equanimity; indeed, the NSDAP and the KPD cooperated from time to time and were even known to share the same offices in some places. Stalin thought that the Second World War would be a re-run of the First, with the European powers becoming bogged down. When they had exhausted themselves the USSR would be free to intervene and do as she pleased. Again, this was a disastrous miscalculation. All the USSR succeeded in doing was to make Germany even stronger. A Machiavelli might argue that in the end it all turned out right for the Soviet Union. Not only was Germany defeated but Moscow ended up occupying part of Germany, thereby making the USSR a great power. This, however, is no justification for a policy which unleashed a holocaust which killed over fifty million and maimed millions of others in body and mind. Also, this argument assumes that the Soviet occupation of eastern Europe was a net benefit to Moscow. All the European powers must assume some responsibility for the outbreak of hostilities, but had France, Great Britain and the Soviet Union acted decisively together in 1939, Germany could not have launched a European and eventually a world war.

STALINISM TRIUMPHANT

Stalinism flowered in a responsive soil. Without his army of willing cohorts, Stalin could not have propelled the Soviet Union into breakneck industrialisation and collectivisation and maintained the pace after the initial enthusiasm had ebbed. A corps of state and party officials came into being who were welded to the Stalin chariot [129]. The bloodletting and the violence of collectivisation found many wanting, and they passed from the scene and were replaced by those who were not so squeamish. Battle-scarred, ruthless and dedicated, the new men really were people of a special mould. Since their goal was socialism, any measure which advanced the USSR towards that glorious culmination was justified. If mistakes were made they paled into insignificance when placed alongside the triumphs of the period. Since capitalism had been left behind, what was being built in the USSR had to be socialism.

What were Stalin's aims during the 1930s? Simply to make

the Soviet Union politically, economically and militarily strong. The greater the industrial growth, the stronger the USSR became. The terror was used to produce a pliable, malleable work force, to destroy opposition to central directives, to render everyone insecure, from the top official to the collective farmer, and to shift blame for all the shortcomings of everyday life on to the shoulders of those arrested and sentenced.

The typical Stalinist official was of peasant origin. He eagerly followed the party leadership and quickly accepted the view that all opinions which differed from those of the leadership were treasonous. The XVIIth Party Congress in 1934 can be seen as a watershed. Eighty per cent of the delegates had joined the party before 1920 and hence really belonged to the Leninist élite. At the Congress, however, Stalin secured the abolition of Rabkrin,* the Workers' and Peasants' Inspectorate, which supervised government officials, and of the Central Control Commission, which was responsible for party officials. This breakthrough, allied to Kirov's murder, opened the floodgates of violence. The purges swept most of the Leninist élite to their doom. They were replaced in turn by the Stalinist élite. Some of the Stalinist cadres were motivated by idealism, some were attracted by the perquisites of office [*Doc. 15*], others by the feeling of power which their position afforded them.

Stalin liked military metaphors. He referred to the party as the General Staff of the proletariat (*Doc. 1*). At a CC plenum in March 1937 he divided the party into leaders and the led. There were 3,000–4,000 senior leaders, who were the generals; the 30,000–40,000 middle-rank officials made up the officer corps, and the 100,000–150,000 lower-level leaders were the NCOs. This neatly illustrates Stalin's hierarchical way of thinking. No one had any right to an opinion unless his seniority entitled him to one. Stalin's attitude to people was the reverse of the story he told about the incident in Siberia [*Doc. 16*]. In practice he was just as callous or fatalist as the Siberians.

The way Stalin projected himself is instructive. During the 1920s he claimed to be the only true apostle of Lenin; others, such as Trotsky and Zinoviev, were anti-Leninists. Gradually, Stalin became the equal of Lenin, and the phrase 'Lenin–Stalin' made its appearance. The slogan 'Stalin is the Lenin of today' marked the next stage, in which Stalin was ahead of Lenin. Stalin was projected as the father of the nation and the epithet 'Stalinist' guaranteed success. He could work miracles and his intervention produced exaltation and joy [*Doc. 17*]. So successful was the projection of this image [*Doc. 18*] that many people accepted it and believed that all the injustices of the 1930s were the fault of nasty and incompetent officials. Some went to their deaths convinced that if only comrade Stalin had known what was really going on he would have stepped in to right the injustice.

Stalin's rise meant that the role of the party changed. It was no longer true that the party knew best. Stalin's thought became the fount of all wisdom.

There was an assault on learning after 1928 so as to destroy the influence and power of the 'old' élites [125]. They were replaced by new élites whose attitude to learning was radically different. All intellectual activity was to be channelled into fighting the battle for socialism. Learning was demystified, and anyone with the right attitude, a Stalinist attitude, could become a specialist. Folk heroes appeared in many fields: Makarenko in education, Vilyams in grassland management, Lysenko in agrobiology, Marr in linguistics and Michurin in fruit-farming. The fact that practically everything they preached was dismissed out of hand in the west only strengthened their position. What else could one expect from bourgeois scientists jealous of the successes of socialism?

Hence Stalinism meant modernisation, it meant technology, it meant a bright future, it meant victory. The tide of Russian nationalism also rose as national self-adulation increased. This, as has been mentioned, spelled doom for the non-Russian élites.

How did Stalin's state function? The twin pillars of power were the party and the government. The party acted as a parallel government and checked on the implementation of the plans. The flow of information was restricted. The more important an official, the more he was told. The party watched the government, but the political police watched both. Key decision-making was centred in Stalin's own chancellery, presided over by a trusted official, Poskrebyshev. All the threads came together in the chancellery, all the information was pieced together there, the jigsaw was complete. Stalin was the only person in the entire country who saw the whole picture and he skilfully used the information available to him. Stalin's power was not based on control of the government or the party or the political police. It involved exploiting all three. It was vital to Stalin that he should maintain several independent sources of information; in that way he hoped to judge which source was misleading. After 1936 he successfully prevented any body, be it the Politburo or the CC of the party or the government, meeting as a group and taking counsel together independent of him. He preferred to consult individuals or small groups, and here his tactics were based on setting one person against another. This explains why there were only two Party Congresses between 1934 and 1953, for they were frankly unnecessary. Stalin very seldom left Moscow. He disliked mass meetings and was always conscious of his Georgian accent. He restricted the number of people who had direct access to him and in so doing created a mystique around his person.

Why and how did Stalinism function? The destruction of the old ruling strata, the more able farmers, the *kulaks* and the old intelligentsia left a void. It was inevitable that the authoritarian political culture which was just being challenged by civil society (autonomous institutions outside the control of the government) and the new élites (industrialists, lawyers and so on) before 1914 should reassert itself. Lenin changed his views on the state, moving from a weak to a strong state. This fitted the pre-1917 Russian tradition. Autonomous labour organisations, such as factory committees and trade unions, were emasculated because they wished to share in decision-making. No independent institutions were permitted to emerge. Hence all the new institutions and organisations were instrumental, to serve Bolshevik, later Stalinist, goals. The Soviet constitution afforded soviets legislative and executive functions but this constitution was at variance with the newly emerging Bolshevik state. The failure of world revolution isolated Soviet Russia and it had to survive on its own. Outside ideas, 'bourgeois' ideas, were by definition counter-revolutionary. The violent internecine strife which illuminated the 1920s encouraged authoritarianism. Utopianism was given its head during the first Five-Year Plan and led to untold misery for millions of peasants and others. Bukharin, perceptively, warned of the 'Leviathan state' which would emanate from the 'military-feudal exploitation of the peasantry'. The Bolsheviks were determined to eliminate the peasant *mir** or community. The *muzhik** had to depart the stage.

The type of economic planning adopted shaped the regime. Bolshevik rejection of the market was total and this was in part due to the fact that the market was only just emerging in Russia in 1914. Communist planners declined to base their plans on value and price and concentrated on material balances instead. The former would have afforded enterprises the opportunity, in their own interests, to achieve the plan more effectively by cutting costs. Costs, in fact, were ignored in the early years of the first FYP. Material balances meant that an increasing number of quantitative goals, which could not encapsulate quality and innovation, had to be set, thereby requiring more and more bureaucrats. Stalin, significantly, complained of the difficulty of obtaining objective information about enterprise potential during the 1930s. Planners were reduced to increasing annual targets by a certain amount (the ratchet principle). Stalin was forced to legalise the market, but only the *kolkhoz* market. Illegal markets began to develop to make up for the lacunae which the planners could not or would not cope with.

The reasons for the purges are still unclear. Lewin sees them as a means of demonologising the opposition, the majority of the population [90]. Such were the tensions within society, a predominantly peasant society, that Stalin and his co-leaders adopted a peasant idiom. By so doing they hoped to deflect peasant anger at prevailing conditions away from the regime. The purges go through various stages. There are Show Trials. There are purges of local officials with locals being encouraged to denounce local bureaucrats and vent their anger on them. Mobilisation becomes significant in proletarianising the bureaucracy. The same is true of industry.

Recent research [79] does not attempt to provide a monocausal reason for the purges. The totalitarian approach which views the purges as the logical consequences of Marxist–Leninist doctrine, as a product of the inner logic of absolute rule and utopia in power, has not been confronted with a powerful counter-argument. What is clear, however, is that the social scope of the purges appears to be more restricted and less indiscriminate than previously thought. Research now concentrates on how the purges were implemented. Viola (in [79]) demonstrates that the purges in the countryside appear to have revitalised among peasants old methods of disposing of socially marginal persons in the villages. Rittersporn (in [79]) wonders if the recurring theme of conspiracy in Stalinist politics may have been a psycho-social consequence of the structure of power itself. Since power was mainly structured along personal and institutional networks of loyalties, party and state bureaucrats were predisposed to perceiving intra-bureaucratic conflict as conspiracy. The purges affected industrial workers to a much lesser degree than managers and technical personnel. Stakhanovism was pugnacious populism and contained elements of social demagogy. Previous research did not notice that in the armed forces there was a move to expel all officers from the party, which was independent of the arrests and executions. Getty (in [79]) suggests several different explanations for the purges but concludes that there may not have been any identifiable aims at all when Stalin took the decision to initiate them. (This would appear quite erroneous since Stalin devoted great attention to whom should be purged, at least at the top.)

The mass mobilisation and the assault on established élites and bureaucracies are reminiscent of the Cultural Revolution in China, which began in 1966 and was aimed at removing bureaucrats and indeed everyone in authority so as to introduce new cohorts who would be more responsive to the thoughts of Chairman Mao. It is as if the Stalin leadership were dissatisfied with the new bureaucratic élites which emerged. They had to be swept away to make way for new cohorts which in turn would be decimated. The party-state became more and more dependent on its bureaucrats as the economy grew but, ironically, the iconoclastic attitude to local officials meant that they could not be relied upon to implement orders. The low level of expertise was part of the problem, but the other aspect was the impossible demands visited on local officials and managers. They, in turn, developed defence mechanisms, including colluding to report overblown successes, to such an extent that a permanent tension developed between the centre and the periphery. The centre reacted by attempting to eliminate horizontal links and networks.

For example, in 1934 the existing economic regions were divided into 79 smaller *oblasts*, the principal territorial subdivision of a republic, plus the cities of Moscow and Leningrad. Between 1934 and 1944 Urals *oblast*, which had developed into an economic and political centre to rival Moscow, was split into six new *oblasts*. What did this restructuring of the economic administration lead to? To the destruction of established structures, to the reshuffling of personnel, to the violation of economic and cultural life. It undermined specialisation and cooperation. One of the reasons why Aleksei Rykov, a former chairman of *Sovnarkom*, was executed was because he had argued that the economy could not be run from the centre. The same happened in the northern regions. The whole Arctic region was divided among the central ministries so that no central body existed to control the colonisation of the north. Thus, the northern minorities lost all control over their own existence. The great central ministries attempted to gain control over all enterprises within their remit. However, it is doubtful if the ministries at the centre could have been effectively coordinated.

Hence Stalinism flowered for a short time but sowed the seeds of its own impotence. Bent on destroying local autonomy, especially in non-Russian areas, it was not able to put anything dynamic in its place. The late 1930s saw the gradual decline of Stalinism.

3 THE GREAT FATHERLAND WAR, 1941–45

THE ATTACK

Operation Barbarossa (Red Beard) was launched at 4.00 (Moscow time) on the morning of Sunday 22 June 1941 across a wide front. There were three main groups to the German attack. Army Group North headed for the Baltic States and Leningrad, Army Group Centre struck towards Belorussia and Moscow, and Army Group South thrust towards Ukraine and Kiev. The *Wehrmacht* had 3.2 million men at its disposal and Finnish, Hungarian, Slovak, Romanian, Italian and Spanish troops joined in later [5].

The Red Army, numbering some 2.9 million men, and the Red Air Force were quite unprepared for the onslaught. Despite precise information about the imminent attack from defecting German soldiers and the British government – both ignored – front commanders were under strict instructions not to take any action. Hence when the Germans attacked they had to ask for orders.

Stalin was stunned by the turns of events. Just why he should have trusted Hitler to keep to the terms of the Non-Aggression Pact and not attack the USSR has never been satisfactorily explained. It is all the more puzzling given his suspiciousness, verging on paranoia, of the motives and actions of Soviet citizens. It would appear that Molotov was the *de facto* leader of the country during 22–30 June 1941 as Stalin lay in a state of shock at his dacha outside Moscow. Had his subordinates decided that they had had enough of the dictator, he could surely have been eliminated. They obviously came to the conclusion that Stalin was irreplaceable and that the country desperately needed him.

Two bodies were set up to fight the war. A General Staff, *Stavka*,* was appointed on 23 June, with responsibility for all land, sea and air operations. The more important body, the State Committee of Defence (GKO),* appeared on 30 June. It had a wider brief, supervising the military, political and economic life of the country.

Stalin had sufficiently composed himself by 3 July 1941 to address the nation and to tell the terrible truth about the war [*Doc. 19*]. He appealed to everyone in the name of Mother Russia to fight the invader to the death. If the Red Army was forced to retreat, nothing of any value was to be left for the invader. A scorched earth policy was to be carried out.

GERMAN WAR GOALS

The Germans did not invade the Soviet Union because they feared imminent attack. It was thus not a preventive war on their part, but a continuation of the policy of aggression pursued since 1938. The immediate target was to attain a line running from Archangel to Astrakhan. From there German bombers could hit industrial targets in the Urals. This was not to be an ordinary occupation: communism was seen by Hitler as the main obstacle to his plans for world domination and the Soviet Union had all the raw materials and living space, *Lebensraum*, that Germany needed. The Russians were to be 'severely beaten' and reduced to a 'leaderless people performing labour'. Since socialism in the Soviet Union was ineradicable, the USSR was to be broken up into separate socialist states which would be dependent on Germany. A 'national Russian state' was not to be allowed to exist since it would inevitably be anti-German. The *Wehrmacht* was given orders to be ruthless: 'We are not waging war to conserve the enemy', declared the Führer. Himmler, head of the SS (*Schutzstaffel* or protection units), was even more frank: 'I am totally indifferent to the fate of the Russians and Czechs. ... Whether they live well or are wracked by hunger only interests me in so far as we need them as slaves for our culture. Otherwise they don't interest me.' The *Generalplan Ost* stipulated that about 75 per cent of the Slav population was to be moved later to Siberia. Germans, Norwegians, Swedes, Danes and Dutch were to colonise the land vacated by the Slavs.

In the Caucasus the *Wehrmacht* supported national governments, which sprang up in the wake of the retreating Red Army. A Karachai national government, for instance, came into being. The experiment, however, was not repeated in the Slav areas. This policy was opposed by some German commanders. General Jodl, for example, wanted to appeal to the Russians over the heads of their leaders as a way of breaking up the Soviet Union.

THE PROGRESS OF THE WAR

The *Wehrmacht* knew that it could not conquer and occupy the whole of the Soviet Union. It needed to defeat the Red Army in a *Blitzkrieg*, a lightning war. The resources of the country in men and war material were so enormous that a long-drawn-out encounter would most likely favour the Soviets. Hence the tactics were to advance rapidly and encircle and destroy huge concentrations of men and equipment. This required great mobility and almost total control of the air. This the *Luftwaffe* had secured early on. The Soviet forces' main hope was to slow down the German advance. Every hold-up, every hour's delay, gave more time for an effective defence to be organised. Hence Stalin's appeal for every citizen to defend Mother Russia to the last drop of blood [*Doc. 19*].

The first stage of Operation Barbarossa was completed successfully but then the Germans hesitated. Hitler thought of striking at Leningrad, the General Staff wanted to push on to Moscow, but on 21 August Hitler surprised everyone by deciding to go south to take Ukraine. There the *Wehrmacht* could live off the land, which it could not do in the north. Then, on 17 September 1941, with Leningrad at his mercy, Hitler withdrew his armour and bombers to strengthen the forces in the south in their bid to take the Crimea and the Baku oilfields. Leningrad was now to be starved into submission.

By 26 September 1941 over half a million Germans, or one in six on the eastern front, had been killed or wounded. Then Hitler decided to attack Moscow, and on 30 September 1941 he launched 'Operation Typhoon'. As the advance German units reached the outskirts of the capital, Stalin panicked again. On the night of 16–17 October he left, but returned the next day. Meanwhile the underground stopped, the NKVD and police left the streets, the bakeries stopped producing bread, and the communists tore up their party cards. Incredibly the Germans did not realise this, and once gone the opportunity never recurred.

The Red Army counter-attacked during the night of 5 December 1941 and when it discovered how weak the German defences were, it launched an offensive over a 1,000 kilometre front. Had Hitler not demanded that every German soldier hold his ground, disaster might have overtaken the *Wehrmacht*. Even so it was thrown back 200–300 kilometres in places.

The successful defence of Moscow was due in large part to the incisive leadership of Zhukov. He was fortunate to have some fresh Siberian troops at his disposal and he held them back until they could have the maximum effect. Stalin had been able to withdraw about half his Far Eastern troops, together with about 1,000 tanks and 1,000 aircraft, to bolster the capital's defences. The vital information which permitted this move came from Richard Sorge, a German communist spy in Tokyo, who had discovered that the Japanese were not going to strike against Siberia but against the US in the east and the British and French in the south. Had Japan decided to attack Siberia from her base in northern China it is difficult to see how the Soviet Union could have survived. Hitler had not even informed Japan of the planned attack on 22 June 1941. His reason was that he did not wish Japan to share in the glory of routing the Red Army! The Soviet Union was fortunate that the Anti-Comintern Pact only existed on paper and was not a military alliance.

The battle for Moscow was a turning point in the war. Was the failure of the *Blitzkrieg* due more to the *Wehrmacht*'s shortcomings than to the strengths of the Red Army? The Germans were not prepared for a winter war. Hitler had only expected a short campaign, leaving 15–20 divisions in the USSR. The clinging mud meant that tracked vehicles were necessary, but most German vehicles were wheeled. German carts fell apart and their horses died in thousands, while the mangy Russian animal carried on. When the frosts came the Germans had no warm clothing and little anti-freeze for their vehicles; Soviet tanks did not need this since they ran on diesel. Jackboots offered little protection at −30°C, and between 27 November 1941 and 31 March 1942 over a quarter of a million German soldiers succumbed to frostbite.

German estimates of Soviet strength were woefully inaccurate. Yet even had his generals come up with correct estimates Hitler would have dismissed them out of hand as being pro-Soviet. He had an *idée fixe* about Slavs being *Untermenschen*, or inferior beings, and was unwilling to alter his opinion in the light of contrary information. The Germans committed many tactical mistakes. If they had taken Moscow, this would have put the nerve centre of the country out of action since all communications went through the capital. Leningrad, the city of Lenin and of revolution, would also have been a great psychological victory.

The *Wehrmacht* believed itself so strong that it did not concern itself with the political war. The 'commissar order' of 6 June 1941, which required every Red Army political commissar to be shot, was short-sighted and criminal. It was soon extended to include other party and government officials, and also Jews. About two million

Soviet prisoners were taken in the first year of the war and this revealed how low Russian morale was. The Germans were quite unprepared for such numbers and many of the prisoners died of hunger and disease. Of the 5.7 million Soviet prisoners taken during the war 3.4 million died in captivity [*Doc. 19*]; about one million Germans died in Soviet camps.

Allowing prisoners of war to die was self-defeating since it stiffened Soviet resolve, and the propaganda about death awaiting every Red Army man who surrendered turned out to contain much truth. Many non-Russians had welcomed the Germans as liberators, preferring them to Soviet rule, but the Germans squandered this goodwill by their brutality.

However, German mistakes in 1941 pale into insignificance when compared to their successes. In the short run everything favoured the Germans. Neither Stalin nor the General Staff, *Stavka*,* possessed any knowledge of modern warfare. They had to learn in the field, but this was costly, although eventually the lessons learnt were put to good effect. The price for Stalin's slaughter of the top echelons of the army had now to be paid. However, Stalin must be given credit for many of his principal appointments, especially that of Marshal Zhukov, who became commander of the western front in October 1941. He was given his head and eventually won Stalin's grudging admiration. During the first year of the war commanders could display more initiative than later.

During 1942 the *Wehrmacht* scored triumph after triumph, but victory was becoming increasingly difficult to achieve. In June 1942 Hitler launched his troops against Stalingrad, but near the city he split his forces, half to take the town, the other half to go southwards towards Baku. By early September German and Soviet troops were fighting in the streets of Stalingrad and one of the epic battles of history ensued. The *Wehrmacht* was tantalisingly close to victory on several occasions but the self-sacrifice and heroism of the defenders turned the tide. Hitler would not allow the Sixth Army to make a tactical retreat so as to avoid being encircled in a counter-attack, and he thereby sealed its fate. Romanian, Hungarian and Italian troops, whom the Red Army found easier to fight than the Germans, were cut to shreds. Field-Marshal Paulus and twenty-four generals surrendered, along with some 90,000 men. About 200,000 Germans perished in the ruins of Stalingrad; Soviet losses will never be known.

Stalingrad was a turning point. For the first time the Soviets had defeated the German army in a pitched battle and the psychological effect was immense. The *Wehrmacht* was not invincible after all. Yet from the German point of view the battle had been unnecessary. Stalingrad was not of primary stategic importance, for the Volga could have been cut between the city and Astrakhan with the same effect and minimal loss.

The initiative, however, still lay with the *Wehrmacht*, and it decided to repair its reputation in the east. Hitler chose Kursk and committed all his heavy tanks to what became the greatest tank battle in history to that date. The Soviets made a similar commitment, and when they discovered the exact time of the attack, on the morning of 4 July 1943, struck first and put a significant number of German guns out of action. On 13 July Hitler broke off the engagement after the *Wehrmacht* had failed on several occasions to achieve a decisive breakthrough. Kursk, therefore, was also a turning point. The tactical initiative now passed to the Red Army.

As the tide slowly turned, the way was open for the advance on Berlin. This was checked from time to time but in the end became irresistible. The year 1944 saw a complete transformation of the situation. By late March the Soviets were approaching Czechoslovakia and Romania. A tremendous Soviet offensive was launched on 22 June 1944 over a 700-kilometre front, just two weeks after the successful Anglo-American landings in Normandy. The *Wehrmacht*'s losses mounted alarmingly and its performance between June 1944 and May 1945 was poor, except for the struggle to hold East Prussia. The Soviets did not make a beeline for Berlin. They switched troops to the south to assist the push into the Balkans. Romania was separated from Germany in August 1944 and war was declared on Bulgaria, although technically the country had never declared war on the Soviet Union. In the course of the autumn the Red Army also penetrated into Hungary and Yugoslavia.

Why was it that the German forces did so well until Kursk and then fell away; or to phrase the question differently, why did the Red Army prove irresistible after July 1943?

The Germans started off with the incalculable benefit of tactical surprise. Man for man they were better than the Soviets and so was their equipment. This gradually changed as Stalin and his generals learned how to fight a modern war, and the Soviet success in the tank battle of Kursk demonstrated that they had mastered the art. The *Luftwaffe* controlled the skies in the early stages but a war has to be won on the ground. The Soviets were prepared to sustain heavy losses for tactical gain. Whereas German personnel could not be replaced (the *Wehrmacht* was already short of 625,000 men by April 1942) the Soviets had abundant reserves (but even so were running short in 1945). The vaunted German military discipline proved a disadvantage when things started to go badly. The *Wehrmacht*'s chain of command was strictly hierarchical, with unquestionable orders handed down from above. Such a system is fine if the supreme commander is providing first-class leadership, but Hitler made too many mistakes. Seasoned commanders would arrive at the Führer's HQ telling themselves that they were going to put Hitler right, and would leave on cloud seven believing a miracle was about to occur. The personal oath of loyalty which officers swore to Hitler inhibited the vast majority from acting decisively against him. The German military system did not produce men who would put their country first and everything else second. Tactically, the Germans were very rigid. As the war progressed, the Red Army learned to anticipate the moves the Germans were likely to make and were thus able to counter them more and more effectively. German NCOs were not trained to use their own initiative; hence, by the end of the war, the *Wehrmacht* was almost incapable of springing a tactical surprise. Given their experience and resources the Germans should have performed much better after June 1944. Even their most bitter enemies were surprised by the speed with which the great German war machine broke down.

The Red Army only fought on one front, while the *Wehrmacht* was engaged on several. Things became more difficult for the Germans after the Anglo-American landings in North Africa in November 1942. Thereafter Hitler had constantly to switch his resources. Troops had to be kept in France to guard against an Allied landing there, and as it turned out too many men were stationed in France at a time when they were desperately needed on the eastern front. One of the reasons which led Hitler to pull out of the battle of Kursk was the news of the Allied landings in Sicily.

Lend-Lease* aid was important, despite the efforts of Soviet writers to play down its significance. Khrushchev, once out of office, revealed how important American Dodge trucks and gun mountings had been to the Soviet war effort [11]. They helped to make the Red Army mobile in 1943 and speeded up its advance. But the main contribution to the supply of war material was made by Soviet industry. Prodigious achievements were recorded as the whole nation was girded for war; the result was that the Soviet war machine gradually out-produced the German, and the longer the war lasted the greater the difference became. For instance, the

Soviets produced twice as many rifles and sub-machine guns as the Germans during the war and finally out-produced them in every major category of weapon. Some of the Soviet material was superior to the German from the very beginning; this applied especially to certain types of tank and to the Katyusha rocket.

Morale and willpower are always very important during wartime. During 1941 the Red Army either fought very poorly or just surrendered. This rapidly changed, and after Stalingrad Soviet morale was very high. The Germans made life more difficult for themselves because of their brutality and their maltreatment of prisoners. They made the war a savage one from the start. The Red Army paid them back in kind and gradually the German soldier began to fear 'Ivan', as the Soviet soldier was known. If a German soldier misbehaved himself elsewhere he was sent to the eastern front as a punishment. The average Soviet soldier was better able physically to endure war than the German.

The number of Soviet war losses has always been an emotive and controversial issue. Stalin, in March 1946, put the figure at 7 million but Khrushchev raised it to 20 million. Gorbachev, on the 45th anniversary of the war's end in 1990 announced that research had produced a figure of 26–27 million. In 1993 it was estimated that military losses during the war were 8.7 million, of whom 289,000 died from accidents or were executed by the Red Army [73]. Corrections to these figures provide another estimate: 7.8 million dead, of whom 5.5 million died at the front, 1.1 million from wounds in hospital, and 1.2 million in German captivity [73].

THE ECONOMY

By November 1941 about half the population and one-third of productive capacity had been lost or was threatened. Enormous efforts were made to dismantle factories and by November 1941 over 1,500 had been moved eastwards. Women and the unskilled had to be used to fill the gaps left by the fighting men, but they succeeded in raising production in 1942 to 59 per cent and by 1944 to 79 per cent of the GDP in 1940 [70].

Food production suffered, as much of the arable land fell under German control. Grain output in 1942 was 36 per cent and in 1944 64 per cent of that of 1940. Horses, where available, were sent to the army, so that women, who had to shoulder most of the burden, were left to farm under the most primitive conditions. Where there were no animals, women had to be yoked to the plough. The cow population in 1942 was only half that of 1940. The Soviet Union simply went hungry during the war years [*Doc. 20*].

CULTURE

The two years which followed the invasion were an Indian summer for Soviet letters. A torrent of writing about the war engulfed the reader. Deeply patriotic and violently anti-German, it painted a picture of fortitude, heroism, self-sacrifice and suffering. The long agony of the Leningrad siege – when the terrible winter of 1941–42 claimed 600,000 civilian deaths, mostly the result of starvation and cold – produced particularly moving literature. The common soldier was not forgotten and his qualities of wit, humour and perseverance were celebrated in print and on the stage.

Someone had to be held responsible for the dreadfully poor leadership of the Red Army, and in his novel *The Front*, published in *Pravda* in August 1942, Aleksandr Korneichuk put the blame fairly and squarely on the shoulders of the older generation of war leaders. The younger generation, more technically able, would, he asserted, turn the tide.

Russia's national history was glorified and the heroes of the past who had served Russia at vital moments – Aleksandr Nevsky, Kutuzov, Peter the Great and the like – rallied the forces again from the grave. This glorification of the past continued a trend which had already been perceptible in the 1930s.

Writers had great leeway when it came to deciding how to treat their subjects, but in late 1943 the party began again to exert some authority. The person who felt the full force of the party's ire was Mikhail Zoshchenko, a noted satirist. His *Before Sunrise* was stated to be too pessimistic, too subjective and short on patriotism. Konstantin Fedin also came in for some harsh treatment. The offending work was volume two of his Gorky anthology, and such was the furore that volume three was never published.

Writers seized the opportunity afforded them by the war of depicting real people in real situations. Heroes and heroines came to life on the page and were a far cry from the nebulous beings of the late 1930s.

THE PARTY

The war changed the composition of the party. During it over five million candidate members and 3.6 million new members joined the ranks of the party; of these, 3.9 million candidate members and 2.5 million members were serving in the army and navy. By 1945 one-quarter of the men and women in the armed forces were communists and a further 20 per cent were members of the *Komsomol*. This meant that service men and women accounted for just over half of party members at the end of the war. This was a new phenomenon, for in June 1941 only 15 per cent of the military had been enrolled in the party.

THE NATIONALITIES

The multinational nature of the Soviet Union was a potential weakness on the eve of the German invasion [120]. The decimation of the national élites during the purges and the travails of collectivisation had left behind a reservoir of resentment among many non-Russians. Stalin did not afford Soviet Germans the luxury of choice. He dissolved the Volga German autonomous republic in August 1941 and packed off all the Germans, communists included, to the east [*Doc. 21*].

Since some nationalities welcomed the German invaders, they were accused of collaboration and deported. This involved the Karachai in October–November 1943, the Kalmyks in December 1943, the Chechens and Ingushi in February 1944, the Crimean Tatars in June 1944, the Greeks also in 1944, as well as the Meskhetians and the Balkars (though there is some doubt about the date in the case of the last two). In all, about 3.3 million people were deported   or resettled between 1941 and 1948. All these nations were rehabilitated after 1956, demonstrating the fact that their suffering had been for nothing. After rehabilitation these nationalities were allowed to return to their ancestral homes with two exceptions, the Volga Germans and the Crimean Tatars. Some Germans, however, left the Soviet Union to settle in East or West Germany.

THE GRAND ALLIANCE

No formal alliance involving Great Britain, the USA and the USSR was ever concluded. When Winston Churchill heard of the German attack he moved quickly to propose aid to the Soviet Union. There was no immediate response from the Soviet side, but with Stalin back at the helm everything changed. An Anglo-Soviet diplomatic agreement was reached on 12 July 1941, and on 18 July Stalin wrote to Churchill proposing a second front in France and another in the Arctic. When the Soviet leader met Harry Hopkins, President Roosevelt's personal envoy, at the end of July, he had already drawn up a long list of needed equipment. On 3 September 1941 Stalin asked Churchill for 30,000 tonnes of aluminium by the beginning of October and a minimum *monthly* aid of 400 aeroplanes and 500 tanks. He also wanted a second front in the Balkans and France in 1941. On 13th September 1941 he proposed that Great Britain should land 25–30 divisions at Archangel or ship them to the southern part of the USSR via Iran to cooperate militarily on Soviet soil with the Red Army. Asking for foreign troops on Soviet soil underlines how desperately pessimistic Stalin was about the situation. The US extended a $1,000 million credit in November 1941 and included the USSR in the Lend-Lease Act [5].

Hitler committed a major error of judgement when he declared war on America on 11 December 1941. Had he not done so it is more than possible that the USA would have restricted herself to fighting Japan before committing combat troops to the European theatre.

An Anglo-Soviet treaty was signed in London on 26 May 1942 but it had taken six months to negotiate. One sticking-point was that the Soviets wanted the frontiers of 22 June 1941 to be recognised. This would have meant Poland ceding territory, but the Polish government-in-exile in London would countenance no such thing. The Americans were also against making binding agreements about post-war frontiers. This highlighted the problem of Poland, which was to become one of the most bitter during the war. Even when the Soviet Union was waging a life and death struggle with the *Wehrmacht*, Stalin was still thinking about future territorial gains.

One of the few occasions on which Stalin lost his temper in the presence of a western statesman was in August 1942 in Moscow, when Churchill informed him that Anglo-American forces would not invade northern France but North Africa in November 1942. Stalin's reaction was to taunt Churchill with the suggestion that British troops were afraid of fighting Germans. The British Prime Minister swallowed this insult. Indeed, on the Anglo-American side there were some feelings of guilt about the fact that it was the Red Army which was bearing the brunt of the *Wehrmacht*'s onslaught. Stalingrad was a turning point in relations. Until then the Soviet Union had been begging for aid and was very fearful of the future. Afterwards, as the tide of war began to turn, Stalin became very self-confident in his dealings with Allied statesmen. He knew that time was on his side and that if the Red Army overran eastern Europe it would be Moscow which would decide the shape of the western frontiers of the Soviet Union.

The first time the Big Three – the UK, the USA and the USSR – came together was at Tehran in November 1943, and it was a striking success for Soviet diplomatic skill as Churchill and Roosevelt competed with one another to please Stalin. They did not take a firm line on Poland, and indeed it was Churchill who suggested that perhaps Poland could be compensated for loss of land in the east by the acquisition of some German territory in the west. The second front in France was firmly set for 1944.

By the time the Big Three met again at Yalta, in the Crimea, in February 1945, the military situation had so changed that the USSR was preparing the final assault on Berlin. Eastern and south-eastern Europe had been almost completely overrun. Finland had left the war in September 1944. A Polish provisional government had been recognised by Moscow on 5 January 1945. In May 1944 Churchill had conceded the Soviet Union a key role in Romania and Bulgaria, and when he visited Moscow in October 1944 he widened the agreement to embrace Hungary and Yugoslavia, in which countries the USSR and the west were to have equal influence. Greece was to fall within the British sphere [5]. Stalin merely put a large tick against the percentages proposed by the British Prime Minister. Since both parties were aware of the fact that there were no Anglo-American troops in the countries involved, Churchill was tacitly conceding that the Soviets would play the leading role in them. In Greece, British troops were present, and this would tip the scales there.

Although Stalin did not get everything he wanted at Yalta, he could derive some satisfaction from the meeting. The Polish frontier was to be moved westwards, with the final details being worked out at the peace conference after the war. This was guaranteed to make post-war German–Polish relations very tense, with Berlin attempting to recover the lost territories. In such circumstances Poland would need an ally interested in maintaining the new frontier. The USSR could play this role and in so doing bind Poland to herself. Another gain from Yalta was that the Soviet Union was to receive southern Sakhalin and the Kurile islands for going to war with Japan after Germany had been defeated.

Neither side completely trusted the other to fight Germany to a finish. The western Allies were not certain as late as the summer of 1944 whether, once the Red Army reached the German frontier, it would not stop. Stalin, in his turn, suspected that the western Allies might conclude a separate peace with Berlin, thus freeing the *Wehrmacht* to pit all its strength against the Soviet Union. One of the reasons why Churchill was willing to concede so much in 1944–45 was the fear that if some agreement were not reached the victorious Red Army might sweep forward so fast that Moscow would become the arbiter of the fate of all Europe. His concessions to Moscow were an attempt to salvage as much as possible for the west.

The Red flag flying over the *Reichstag* in Berlin on 2 May 1945 symbolised the new situation. The Soviet Union had become the leading power in Europe and was also a world power. It was only later that Moscow and Washington came to accept this. On VE Day, 8 May 1945 (9 May 1945 in Moscow, because of the time difference), the Soviet Union was unsure of herself and uncertain how long she would be staying in Germany. Washington expected the USSR to be economically weak and to need up to twenty years to recover fully. Britain was expected to be the leading power in Europe, but was economically in no position to sustain such a role.

4 HIGH STALINISM, 1945–53

The war raised Stalin's stature to new heights; afterwards he basked in the reflected glory of military success. The years which separate 1945 from his death on 5 March 1953 saw the cult of his personality reach astounding heights. He became the true charismatic leader. There was always an air of mystery about him. He was not given to much internal travel, and Khrushchev maintained that he only knew the country and agriculture from film which, of course, had been deliberately touched up. Stalin was also sparing in his public appearances. In a pre-television era most citizens knew him only from newspaper photographs. The films in which he appeared presented him in heroic colours with no sign of the pock marks on his face. Like many short men – he was only about 1.6 metres in height – he was acutely conscious of the fact, and portraits and films give the deliberate impression of a taller man.

Stalin moved quickly after victory to break up the key institutions which had fought the war and hence wielded great power. The State Defence Committee (GKO) was dissolved on 4 September 1945 and its functions distributed among various commissariats. Demobilisation had begun in June 1945 and the party launched a campaign to raise the ideological level of its members [5]. This was of pressing importance since many members had been enrolled on the battlefield. Since most soldiers were from the countryside their formal education had been modest. The military hierarchy was also downgraded. Marshal Zhukov left Germany for the Odessa Military District and lost his position on the party CC; other high-ranking officers followed him into less important posts. There was practically no promotions to the senior ranks between the end of the war and Stalin's death.

The upper reaches of the party took on a new life. From December 1945 the Politburo began to meet fortnightly. The CC convened in March 1946 and elected a new Politburo, Secretariat and Orgburo.* Shortly afterwards, in August 1946, the Politburo ruled that the Orgburo was to supervise all party affairs and to meet at least once a week. All this did not mean that the supreme organs of the party had been reinvested with the authority they had possessed in the 1920s. Stalin was in name only a secretary of the CC, but in reality he still held the reins of power. As time passed the frequency of meetings decreased. The party favoured a flowering of Marxist–Leninist ideology, but Stalin held back since there was no guarantee that it could be fully kept under control. Ideology was important to Stalin but only as something which was decreed from on high.

Interpreting Stalin's thought was particularly difficult as he was never a man to waste words. There are only three items for 1947 and two for 1949 in his collected works. *Pravda* editorials called for everything to be done in a Stalinist spirit and declared that a Stalinist attitude to work was needed, but all this was not very helpful if one's task was to repair combine harvesters. The worker who discovered the technical solution to a problem was praised for demonstrating Stalinist initiative.

The Americans thought that the war had profoundly changed the USSR. The Comintern had been dissolved in May 1943 and this led many to think that Moscow was giving a low priority to revolution. In reality the USSR did not need the Comintern any more, since it could coordinate communist policy in the CC Secretariat. Washington yearned for a stable world order, with the great powers all pulling together to create a brave new world. Potential trouble spots could be defused by mutual agreement, and no one power would selfishly use international tension for its own ends. There were many idealists in the American government who believed that, if sufficient concessions were made, Moscow would come to see that things had changed and would play the world game according to American rules. Stalin could never bring himself to believe that this offer was genuine. Presumably, had the boot been on the other foot and had the USSR enjoyed an atomic monopoly, Stalin would have squeezed as many concessions out of Washington as he could. So far as he was concerned the American propositions were a trap, since the USA, being so much stronger than the USSR, had no need to offer concessions. In this Stalin was far less perceptive than, for instance, Maxim Litvinov, the former Foreign Minister, who favoured a much more positive approach to the USA.

Had Stalin decided to meet the Americans half way it would have meant dismantling part of the Stalinist system. American technology, capital, ideas, culture and political values would have penetrated the Soviet Union, loosening up the rigid hierarchical structure which was fundamental to Stalinism. The Soviet leader was pessimistic about the capacity of the USSR to resist an inflowing American tide. The origins of the cold war are complex but the fact that the Soviet Union felt herself inferior to the USA is of crucial importance. If the USSR was not a match for the USA then she was certainly not one for the USA and her allies. Moscow could never admit this to itself, or to the world. Hence it was necessary to give the impression that the country was strong and that America was not half so strong as she thought she was. The violence of the verbal polemics testifies to Moscow's nervousness; they bit deep into the American soul, caused great offence, and further exacerbated the situation. Neither Britain nor France took the rhetoric as seriously as America; they had learned from their historical experience and had developed an imperial, not to say imperious, hauteur towards the criticism of others.

Negotiating with the Soviets was seldom a rewarding exercise, for the Soviet Union had practically no experience of the outside world and had few experts and specialists versed in the thought and practices of the capitalist powers. Very little authority was delegated to Soviet negotiators; their brief was to hold on to what the Soviet Union had and attempt to gain further advantage. Soviet negotiators tried to seize the initiative at meetings by exaggerated criticisms of the other side, openly challenging its good faith. This put their opponents on the defensive and forced them to justify themselves – an unpleasant position for people who assumed beforehand that they, and not the Soviets, held the stronger hand. The USSR never brought any good will to the negotiating table, for she took it for granted that her protagonists were out to score off her and to reduce her power. Since the USSR often found herself ranged against France, Great Britain and America, she found no difficulty in believing that the western powers were in collusion against her.

Stalin acquired some diplomatic skill. He was extraordinarily quick at grasping the essentials of a situation, be it political, economic or technical. He could formulate a response very succinctly and was a master of tactics, talents which he had developed in the political infighting of the 1920s. One of his strengths was that he never allowed sentiment to cloud his judgement; he liked Roosevelt, for instance, but this did not distract him from the task of getting the better of him.

Had the Soviet population been given a choice they would have marched along the road of cooperation with the western allies.

Rumours were rife during the war that things were going to be better after victory, and this implied that the Stalinist system was to be modified. However, such thoughts were far from Stalin's mind in 1945; instead, he set out to recreate the atmosphere of the late 1930s. Soviet soldiers who had been in German prison camps were often marched straight off to Siberian labour camps on their return home. Stalin feared two things: that they might turn on him, and that they might contaminate the Soviet population with their experiences. After all, about 800,000 Soviet citizens had served in the German forces during the war. Every prisoner of war was regarded as having let the Soviet Union down.

Stalin pointed the way ahead in a major speech on 9 February 1946. He maintained that victory had demonstrated the vitality of the Soviet social system and of the Soviet state. Industrialisation had proved its worth and without collectivisation the age-old backwardness of agriculture would not have been overcome. He then enumerated the economic targets not for 1950 but for 1960. The future was going to be hard.

Party membership grew slowly and it was only about 20 per cent higher in 1953 than it had been in 1945. The new recruits were first and foremost the decision-makers, the men and women needed to build the USSR; engineers, technicians, members of the intelligentsia, skilled industrial workers and leading cadres in agriculture. Hand in hand with careful selection of new recruits went purges; about 100,000 members were expelled annually during the last years of Stalin.

Intellectually, the Soviet Union turned in on herself after the war, and foreign learning and achievements were scorned. The man who spearheaded this process was Andrei Zhdanov who had been the party leader in Leningrad during the dreadful siege. Literature was the first to be attacked. The journal *Leningrad* was closed down after being accused of publishing material which was 'permeated with the spirit of servility towards everything foreign'. Then Zhdanov called Mikhail Zoshchenko, a leading satirist, the 'scum of the literary world' and declared that he could not decide whether Anna Akhmatova, a leading poetess, was a nun or a whore. 'Kowtowing to the west', or praising anything foreign, was condemned.

The theatre and the cinema came in for similar treatment, and in agriculture T.D. Lysenko played the role of Zhdanov [5]. Philosophy was also harshly criticised.

The object of this exercise was not to convince writers, academics and scientists that Zhdanov's views – and by extension Stalin's – were correct, but to frighten them. It was an assault on the mind. Along with this went the glorification of all things Russian; anything worth discovering had been discovered by a Russian; relativity theory, quantum mechanics and genetics, which had not been fathered by Russians, were derided as nothing more than pseudoscience. Russian nationalism became even more prominent than during the 1930s. It was synonymous with Soviet patriotism and heralded the downgrading of the achievements of the non-Russian nations in the USSR. One group of citizens who came in for much criticism because of the international situation were the Jews. Jewish theatres and journals were closed down and Jewish intellectuals were arrested. The years 1948–53 were black ones indeed for Soviet Jewry [118].

The world communist movement also split in 1948. Tito, the Yugoslav leader, was unceremoniously drummed out of the Communist Information Bureau (Cominform)* in June 1948. The Cominform had been set up at Szklarska Poreba, in Poland, in September 1947 and embraced most communist parties in Europe. Zhdanov had been the main speaker at its founding Congress and had divided the world into two camps, the socialist and the imperialist, with countries such as Indonesia and India outside both. As far as the Soviet Union was concerned, Tito had thought and acted too independently, even though Tito regarded himself as a loyal Stalinist. Stalin thought that he could bring Tito down very quickly and that Yugoslavia would then return to the fold. This did not happen, and in the Soviet view the Yugoslavs passed over into the camp of the enemy.

Zhdanov died in August 1948. This benefited his main political rival, Georgy Malenkov, who soon afterwards became involved in the framing and subsequent execution of leading Leningrad party and Soviet officials, known as the 'Leningrad Affair'. This erupted in July 1949 and proved fatal among others, for M.I. Rodionov, Prime Minister of the RSFSR, and N.A. Voznesensky, the leading economist of the time. Just why all these key officials were executed is still unclear. What is certain is that everyone feared for his political life. There were a considerable number of top party and central government changes and the atmosphere was charged with mutual suspicion and recrimination. People disappeared, denunciations flowed in to the police, and the dreadful, claustro-phobic atmosphere of the late 1930s returned. N.A. Bulganin, Soviet Prime Minister between 1955 and 1958, once confessed to

Khrushchev: 'It has happened that a man goes to Stalin on his invitation as a friend. And when he sits with Stalin he does nor know where he will be sent next, home or to gaol.' When someone was arrested, the usual response was to pour calumny on him. At the same time the cult of Stalin's personality reached new heights [*Doc. 23*].

If Stalin was hard to men, he was equally hard to women. Milovan Djilas, a prominent Yugoslav communist, records a conversation about the misbehaviour of Soviet troops [*Doc. 24*], which shows that Stalin did not spare a thought for the feelings of the victims of their assaults. This was typical of the attitude towards women during Stalin's last years, which was that the apogee of their calling was to bear children. However, with millions of men dead there were simply not enough males to go round. The law was therefore changed and the paternity suit disappeared. Henceforth a man was not to be held legally responsible for offspring born out of wedlock. The literature of this period portrays the problems which occurred when soldiers returned from active service. Women who had filled men's shoes during wartime had simply to step down. The woman who devoted herself completely to the party and neglected her husband and children now became an object of censure. The male was king, and never had the law and the state been so openly on his side.

Djilas thought he perceived a rapid decline in Stalin's mental faculties by 1948 [*Doc. 25*]. If this is true then it would be one explanation for the mayhem which overtook the USSR between 1948 and 1953. There was no love lost between Stalin and the Jews. When his daughter Svetlana fell in love with an older man who happened to be a Jew, Stalin had him labelled a British agent and dispatched him to an Arctic labour camp. It is striking how many of the political opponents he destroyed were Jews – Trotsky, Zinoviev, Kamenev, Sokolnikov, Radek, to name only a few. However, it is not quite true to say that under high Stalinism there were no Jews in the CC; Kaganovich, for instance, was a member.

It was very difficult for top party and government officials to acquire information. The Politburo and CC probably never met as full bodies between 1947 and 1952. Stalin's tactic was to convene small groups to discuss key policy questions and to supervise their implementation. The XIXth Party Congress in October 1952 appears to have been convened on the initiative of the CC, which had met in August. Stalin was not well enough to deliver the main report, so Malenkov stood in for him. Khrushchev, in delivering the

CC report, was very frank about the behaviour of the little Stalins up and down the country. 'There are quite a few officials who consider that they are not subject to the law. Conceited enough to think that they can do as they please, these officials turn the enterprises or institutions under their control into their own fief where they introduce their own "order" and their own "discipline". There are many scandalous practices of this kind wherever such bureaucrats with a party card in their pockets are active.' The Politburo and the Orgburo were abolished. The new supreme body was the Presidium, which contained more than twice as many full and candidate members* as the old Politburo. The CC and the Secretariat also doubled in size. There was an uneasy feeling that the 'old man' was preparing a new purge. Even Molotov's wife was in exile and such was her husband's nervousness that he did not dare to bring the matter up with his leader. The fact that she was Jewish may have had something to do with her disgrace.

The most startling news of the late Stalin era was carried in *Pravda* on 13 January 1953. A 'doctors' plot' had been discovered in the Kremlin medical centre. Most of the specialists, inevitably Jews, were connected with an American Jewish organisation. There were plans afoot, so it was said, to wipe out the top Soviet leadership. Medical murders had been committed, with Zhdanov among the victims, and it was given out that documentary evidence to support all these allegations existed. But on 23 February 1953 the whole campaign was dropped. The reason soon became apparent; Stalin was nearing his end. He suffered a stroke during the night of 1–2 March and died on 5 March 1953. At the time he was struck down his personal physician, Professor Vinogradov, was not at hand. He was in chains in the Lubyanka prison and was being beaten regularly on Stalin's personal orders. Inside a month the 'doctors' plot' was declared to have been a fabrication and the surviving doctors were rehabilitated.

The years 1948–53 saw millions of Soviet citizens on the move. Besides those going to labour camps and into exile there were repeated round-ups of former prisoners and exiles. Legally these persons had served their sentences and were innocent. However, their residence permits could be cancelled and they could be made to move. Local authorities were simply ordered to clear their town of 'suspicious elements'. Anyone with a record fell within this category, as did everyone else the urban authority wanted to be rid of. Possible suspects had to get out of town very quickly to avoid arrest, for neighbours and landladies immediately reported anyone whom they suspected. The only time to move was at night. The family of the ex-prisoner was automatically in disgrace and his wife automatically lost her job. Nadezhda Mandelstam describes one wife who managed to retain her job by concealing her marriage. Her husband, a violinist, kept perpetually on the move up and down the Volga earning a few roubles here and there by giving lessons. Whenever he could he sneaked back to see his wife, after dark of course. He became so skilled at reading political signals that he was never arrested. Had he been a Jew he would almost certainly have been picked up. However, the strain and lack of proper nourishment eventually told on him and he contracted tuberculosis. He could not teach his son to play the violin since he could never go near the boy for fear of giving him the disease.

ECONOMIC POLICY

Material wartime losses were immense: 70,000 villages and 98,000 *kolkhozes* were wholly or partly wiped out; 1,876 *sovkhozes* were destroyed; 17 million head of cattle and 7 million horses were driven away; 65,000 kilometres of railway track were rendered useless, as well as half of all the railway bridges in occupied territory. In the towns 1.2 million homes had been demolished, and 3.5 million in the country [*Doc. 22*]. The fourth FYP (1946–50) set out the way of putting the country back on its feet. Wonders were, in fact, achieved even when account is taken of the way in which the official figures are exaggerated by the continued use of 1926–27 prices [*Doc. 7* no. 5]. The plan for national income – the approximate equivalent of Gross National Product (GNP) in western statistics – was officially fulfilled [no. 1]. However, agriculture suffered from drought in 1946, as well as a dearth of mechanical equipment, and consequently never approached the planned targets [no. 11]. The poor state of the rural sector meant that the movement of young men and women to the cities, in search of employment, was greater than envisaged [nos 16 and 17]. Hence total money wages were far in excess of the plan [no. 18] and real wages did not rise as quickly as intended [no. 19]. Agricultural incomes were miserably low, and large numbers of farmers were saved from starvation only by the possession of a cow [*Doc. 27*]. However, the more effort put into cultivating the private plot and looking after the cow, the less time there was for social labour on the *kolkhoz*. This was a perennial problem for the authorities, and the policy of the late Stalin era was increasingly harsh. Yet as the taxes and procurements on the private plot increased, after 1949, so farmers reduced their output and livestock numbers. This was at a time when food was desperately short and private plots were responsible for half the total output of agriculture.

Now is an opportune moment to take a closer look at Stalinist economic planning [*Doc. 29*]. A unique system evolved in which the impression was given that a master FYP was being carried out. In reality there was no master plan, merely a mass of lower-level plans which the centre tried to coordinate. How could there have been an overall plan if the FYP was adopted only after the beginning of the period during which the plan was meant to operate? The targets for what each enterprise, each steel mill, each power station had to produce, always demanded more than the economy was capable of producing. Hence there had to be a multitude of adjustments, usually in favour of heavy industry. It was quite normal for a factory to receive emendations every day. All economic units throughout the country were really part of one vast company, USSR Limited. Information was therefore of key importance if the centre – Gosplan* and the economic ministries – was to take rational economic descisions. Many of the failures were due to decisions being based on inadequate information. The Stalinist economic system was efficient from the point of view of control; it was also very successful in concentrating resources in key sectors so as to fulfil priority goals; but in all other respects it was very inefficient and wasteful. Giving priority to certain products meant disrupting the whole economy. Labour discipline and labour productivity are closely linked and here the great optimism of the early 1930s proved misplaced. Workers could be frightened into turning up for work but not into consistently giving of their best.

The key economic official was the first secretary, that is the top party man of an *oblast*. The more important the *oblast* was, industrially speaking, the greater the responsibility of its first secretary. These officials needed technical training and most were engineers. Under Stalin the *oblast* first secretary was responsible for everything in his area and hence had considerable power. He could even take technical decisions without consulting the relevant ministry in Moscow. During the war, first secretaries in the Urals and Siberia, areas vital to the Soviet war effort, were expected to coordinate their efforts and they developed close horizontal collaboration. If one got into trouble at the local level the others would come to his aid. N.S. Patolichev, first secretary in Chelyabinsk *oblast* in the Urals and later the USSR Minister for

Foreign Trade, describes such an incident in his memoirs. In 1942 an order signed by Stalin arrived dismissing the top official of the South Urals railway and putting him on trial. Patolichev was convinced of the man's innocence because of his close working relationship with him. As a result he telephoned his two top contacts in Moscow and asked them to intercede with Stalin. They did so, with the result that the official was simply relegated to a minor post. Patolichev eventually secured his reinstatement, and the man in question later became deputy chairman of the USSR State Committee on Foreign Relations. This incident underlines certain realities of Soviet party life. The first secretary of an *oblast* had considerable autonomy of decision and because of his great responsibilities he needed to develop close ties with others in the same position and with those who played key roles in ensuring that economic plans were met. The first secretary, in practice, was more important than some ministers. However, he was almost helpless when dealing with Stalin. Patolichev ran the risk of losing his job for defending the dismissed man. When Patolichev was promoted to the post of CC secretary in 1946 Stalin asked him whom he would like to have as his assistants. He chose three of the secretaries who had worked with him closely in the Urals since he knew and trusted them. Patolichev also approached someone who had worked with him in Yaroslavl *oblast*, his previous post. This episode neatly illustrates how careers could be built in the Soviet Union. If an official linked himself to a rising star he could rise with him; if he was connected with someone who was going down, he was liable to fall with him. The really skilled official was the one who knew when to change horses.

FOREIGN POLICY

The Soviet Union became a world power in 1945 but could not quite believe it. The western Allies recognised that Moscow had legitimate security interests on her western frontiers and accepted that the regimes which came to power in Poland, Czechoslovakia, Hungary, Romania and Bulgaria could not be anti-Soviet. They did not expect them to be communist but anticipated regimes which might contain communists but whose overall outlook would owe more to western political thinking than to Moscow's views on the subject.

The key country as far as the USSR was concerned was Germany. Even if Moscow neutralised eastern and south-eastern Europe it would be to no avail if Germany became hostile once again. Soviet thinking about post-war Germany began as early as 1943 and by 1944 commissions comprising leading members of the Communist Party of Germany (KPD), then in exile in the Soviet Union, were busily working out plans for German development. It was only at Yalta (February 1945) that Stalin knew for certain that the advance of the Red Army would give it control of a part of Germany. The behaviour of the Soviet reparations and dismantling squads, not controlled by the military in the Soviet zone of Germany but directly under Moscow, angered the Germans. This hurt the prospects of the communists, led by Walter Ulbricht, and boosted support for the Social Democrats (SPD). The latter wanted the factories and equipment which were being seized by the Soviets – on the grounds that they had belonged to Nazi criminals – nationalised and used as the base of a socialist economy. At the Potsdam Conference, in July–August 1945, it was agreed that Germany should be denazified, demilitarised and democratised, and that the USSR should get huge reparations, though the exact sum was not determined. Germany was divided into three zones (increased to four when France became an occupying power) and Berlin was given its own control council under three (later four) power control. A major drawback, not clearly seen at the time, was that Berlin was 180 kilometres inside the Soviet zone.

Relations between the USSR and the western Allies in 1945 were good. In 1946, however, they became strained and during and after 1947 they were bad. There were many reasons for this. From early 1946 the western Allies became concerned about the expansion of Soviet power. The event which marked a watershed took place in the Soviet zone in April 1946, when two political parties, the KPD and the SPD, were compelled to unite in the Socialist Unity Party (SED).* This was mainly due to Soviet concern about the popularity of the SPD. The SED was technically an all-German party, but the other occupying powers would not legalise it in their zone. It was the most powerful party in Germany and as such was feared by France, Britain and America. Many social democrats in East Germany and the vast majority of social democrats in West Germany opposed the fusion. One may regard the fusion as a mistake since it produced an issue which could be used against the Soviet Union; it also meant that Marxist socialism or even Christian socialism suddenly became less attractive in West Germany, and this pushed parties to the right, establishing a gulf which had not existed in 1945.

The Soviets pushed through many reforms in their zones without consulting their allies. They were the first to license political parties, again a unilateral decision. Gradually they realised that short of a war the western Allies could not force them into concessions they did not wish to make. They therefore used their zone as a testing ground. If a reform was acceptable there, it was presumably acceptable elsewhere in eastern and south-eastern Europe.

In eastern and south-eastern Europe there were small indigenous communist parties, led in the main by former Moscow émigrés. Had the membership of these parties been free to act they would have gone for a socialist revolution in 1944–45. However, they were held back by Moscow until 1947. The initial Soviet goal was to carry through democratic revolutions involving parliaments and a multi-party system. Tactically this was an astute move, since the countries concerned were very weak economically, and would find it difficult to satisfy the Soviet demand for reparations; had they gone communist all the resentment of the population would have been directed towards local communists and their Soviet protectors. Stalin knew that the indigenous communist parties had to be cleansed of 'sectarians' and 'adventurers', in short of all those elements which would not accept uncritically the tactics which Moscow proposed. It was not only in the east that the Soviet communists held back fraternal parties from attempting to seize power. Western parties were also affected. Moscow considered it prudent at a time when there were American troops in France and Italy not to be seen to be fomenting revolution. This circumspection lasted until 1947, but by then the most propitious moment for revolution had passed. It is reasonable to assume that there was a general directive to all communist parties to collaborate and to work within the parliamentary system but not to attempt a revolution in 1945 and 1946.

The exception to the above rule was the Communist Party of China. There Mao Zedong was wont to adopt his own counsel, and indeed when the People's Republic of China was proclaimed on 1 October 1949 it came as an unpleasant surprise to Stalin. He would have preferred the communists to come to power in Peking when he judged it opportune. He also wanted a Chinese leadership which was willing to follow Moscow's directives to the letter. Mao and his associates were certainly not such men.

The Cominform's task was to supervise the transformation of eastern and south-eastern Europe into people's democracies. This process occupied the period 1947–49, during which the various states gradually adopted Soviet political institutions and became, in effect, satellites of their powerful neighbour and guardian.

The western powers, by 1947, had become alarmed at the expansion of Soviet power. Hitherto it had been assumed that the main task was to contain a resurgent Germany, but by 1947 the west perceived that the Soviet Union posed the main threat. Policy therefore switched from containing Germany to containing the USSR. The Marshall Plan, the Truman Doctrine, promising help to any regime threatened by communists, the fusing of the American and British zones to form Bizonia, and the currency reform which split Germany economically by introducing new money in West Germany in June 1948, were some of the measures adopted. They, in turn, caused Moscow to seek ways of welding the countries of eastern and south-eastern Europe more closely to her. The Berlin Blockade was the Soviet Union's desperate gambit to force the western powers to go back on their currency reform, but it was self-defeating. The blockade increased hostility to Moscow in all zones of Germany and outside. By the time the blockade was lifted in May 1949 the western zones were well on their way to becoming the Federal Republic of Germany. The currency reform was the key event in the division of Germany, but the Berlin Blockade led many opponents of the establishment of a West German state to change their minds.

The Soviet Union's prime need after the war was security. Soviet foreign policy between 1945 and 1953 was a failure if its objective was to prevent the capitalist world uniting against the USSR. The coming into being of the North Atlantic Treaty Organisation (NATO) in 1949 was the western response to a perceived threat from the Soviet Union. Communism was thought to be on the march and had to be kept at bay. Who was responsible for the cold war [160]? All the leading powers bear some responsibility. So far as Russia was concerned, it had been the practice ever since Peter the Great to seek security by extending the land frontiers of the country. This was partly the result of not having a fixed western frontier, although Peter himself practised it against Persia in the early eighteenth century. The Soviets had always been very nervous about relying on the goodwill of their near neighbours and felt that they had to control these countries wherever possible in order to increase their own security. When Moscow took over a contiguous state, the one next to it became the next source of Soviet security needs. In other words Soviet insecurity was such that gradually more and more states had to be brought within the Soviet orbit. Along with this way of thinking went a peculiarly insensitive appreciation of the feelings of small nations, since Moscow's assumption was that Soviet interests must always take precedence.

Having shed blood in the liberation of south and south-eastern Europe, the Soviet Union felt that she had the moral right to a leading role there. Historically the Russians have either played an important role in other Slav states or have seen themselves as the guardians of them. Misunderstandings arose from the fact that the western Allies deliberately refrained from polemics with Stalin during the war since they regarded their primary task as the defeat of fascism. However, in so doing they negotiated poorly, and Roosevelt especially paid little attention to the consequences of the obligations he entered into. If London and Washington had been tougher from the beginning there would almost certainly have been less friction after 1945. The Soviets felt that America, the key capitalist power (since Great Britain could not act on her own without American support), had acknowledged at the various wartime conferences that eastern and south-eastern Europe should come within the Soviet zone of influence. The USSR felt aggrieved when the Americans and the British began trying to wrest the area away from her. The western Allies, in their turn, felt let down, since promises made by the Soviets – for example, the holding of free elections in Poland – had not been kept. The peace treaties with Bulgaria, Romania and Hungary had not provided for occupation forces. Now that they were, in fact, occupied by Red Army units, America felt betrayed and Great Britain, with public opinion now flowing strongly against the Soviets, felt guilty.

When the western Allies failed to achieve their goals by political and diplomatic means, they began to regard the Soviet Union as an opponent, and a very formidable one. The lack of reliable information about the real state of the Soviet economy and military power led to exaggerated fears about Soviet intentions and power. From underestimating Moscow in 1945 Washington swung over to overrating Moscow in and after 1947. The USSR read American intentions correctly in 1945 and assumed that she would be free from attack. This permitted her to demobilise about nine million men, and according to Khrushchev the armed forces had declined to 2.8 million by 1948. Then the Berlin Blockade, the formation of NATO, and the onset of the Korean war led to a build up.

The Soviets felt that they could not make any major concessions, for once the floodgates were open a rout could easily develop. Stalin knew that given a free vote no country would stay within the Soviet orbit – hence his determination to hold on to what had been gained in eastern and south-eastern Europe, and to secure for the Soviet Union a position from which she could only be dislodged by a world war (which was, of course, unthinkable).

PART THREE: ASSESSMENT

Stalin and Stalinism are no more. However, Stalinism still casts its shadow over post-communist Russia. The task of comprehending the extraordinary phenomenon which was Stalinism is just beginning. The various approaches which have emerged over the last 50 years are flawed and incomplete but can provide a foundation for future research. There are two main schools of thought about Stalinism. They can be called the totalitarian and the pluralist, or the intentional and the structural. The totalitarian approach [9; 18; 64; 108] was a response to the beginning of the cold war and held sway until the 1960s. It concentrates on the state and the personality and preferences of Stalin. Totalitarians would not claim that Stalin achieved his goal of a totalitarian state but that their approach is the most fruitful in understanding the phenomenon of Stalinism. The theory of pluralism implies that the state merely acts as referee between competing interests in society. However, in the real world, this is never quite the case. The state, for instance, is responsible for defence, security and foreign affairs, has its own policy preferences since leaders need to build up a constituency so as to be re-elected. If the pluralist approach is deficient so is the totalitarian. The view that the Stalinist state was tightly disciplined and the ruler was able to impose his will on society is now seen to be flawed. Conquest now concedes that totalitarians acknowledge the ineffectiveness of the state and the significance of initiatives from below. Another way of regarding the totalitarians and the pluralists is to borrow terminology from the study of Nazi Germany and call them intentionalists and structuralists. The former view Hitler as a strong leader, determining and imposing his policy agenda. They place most emphasis on politics and ideology. The latter see a semi-chaotic, polycratic power structure fermenting under the monolithic surface of the regime. Some conclude that Hitler was a weak leader. They stress that institutional, economic, social and other pressures shaped the regime.

In Soviet studies the intentionalists are the totalitarians and the structuralists are the social historians. The seminal presentation by the social historians is that of Sheila Fitzpatrick [126]. She views the Stalin era as a dichotomy between the 'revolution from above' and the 'revolution from below', presented in the contrasting views of the totalitarians and the revisionists, the social historians. The totalitarians, she claims, analyse Soviet development in terms of the dichotomy between state and society, with society reacting, seeking to resist, evade, subvert or, through passive resistance, neuter the demands of the state. The object of the state is therefore to mobilise a victimised, weak, inchoate society. Fitzpatrick challenges these views head on and argues that society was dynamic because new hierarchies, new privileges and levels of status, vertical and horizontal cleavages were emerging [126]. State coercion was, in reality, a response to the problems of managing this social fluidity. The indoctrination of society can be interpreted as part and parcel of the process whereby society acquires the training and culture needed in the new era of socialism. Stalinism had some social as well as political dynamics. Social history from below attempts to clarify these processes. The social historians focus not on the 'actions of the state, but the dynamic of relationships between the different social strata and classes; the prevalent social distinctions and their significance in the lives of individuals; the ways in which individuals could improve their status and protect themselves; the various aspects and repercussions of social mobility; and the ways in which some features of the social hierarchy could persist or emerge in spite of, rather than because of, the actions of the regime' [33 *p*. 26]. Another major concern is whether the new élite at the top of the social hierarchy was a ruling class, in the Marxist sense, or whether it was a group with the highest status and economic advantages in society. This approach is called social history to distinguish it from political history which is primarily concerned with the party-state.

A touchstone is the role of terror. For the 'new cohort' the difference between the Stalinist and the normal political process was one of degree rather than quality. The mobility and dynamism of society were such as to devolve almost into anarchy. Rittersporn [45] sees the origins of the terror in the ungovernability of the country due to bureaucratic infighting and centre-periphery conflict. Getty argues that the great purges were not the 'result of a petrified bureaucracy's stamping out dissent and annihilating old radical revolutionaries. In fact, it may have been just the opposite ... a radical, even hysterical *reaction* to bureaucracy. The entrenched officeholders were destroyed from above and below in a chaotic wave of voluntarism and revolutionary puritanism' [78 *p. 206*]. Hence the role of Stalin is de-emphasised. Rittersporn and Getty regard him as just one of the actors who played a role in the drama of factional strife. Others play down his influence by mentioning him only in passing.

Critics of the social historians reject this approach as an attempt to 'de-demonise' Stalin and the Politburo' and make their politics appear 'humdrum' and ordinary – as if the Soviet government were 'just like any other government operating in difficult circumstances'. By deliberately failing to link social to political history these scholars give the impression that one is dealing with the pluralist model of politics, and hence that there exist similarities between Stalinism and pluralist democracy. One critic claims that they are deflecting some of the blame for the brutalities and suffering of the 1930s away from Stalin and apportioning it elsewhere. Their approach is broadly Marxist in that they search for causes in the 'socio-economic base rather than the political-ideological superstructure'. It is interesting that Fitzpatrick excludes Moshe Lewin [146] from her list of the 'new cohort' of social historians, presumably because he does address the problem of the interaction of the social and the political.

What distinguishes the work of the 'new cohort' from that of Lewin? Fitzpatrick researches mass education, social mobility, cultural revolution and a revolutionary continuity spanning from February 1917 until the consummation of the first Five Year Plan; Getty [78] writes of radical tendencies within the party, which sought to bring the bureaucracy under the influence of a mobilised grass roots democracy; Rittersporn [45] too, finds political forces at play that tried to grapple with bureaucratic conservatism; Manning writes of participatory management in the collective farms; Viola [101] of working-class enthusiasm for the collectivisation campaign; and Thurston [147] of the pleasurable as well as grim aspects of everyday life in the 1930s [33]. Broadly speaking, these scholars have radical sympathies. Lewin, on the other hand, regards the 1930s as a disaster of epic proportions as the Stalinist state set up a proliferation of bureaucratic institutions to stabilise the quicksand society it had created by its own destructive campaigns. Whereas Lewin underlines the view that Stalin was an historical demon by providing it with roots in peasant culture, the 'new cohort' regard this demonic nature as a myth.

These social historians draw the fire of revisionist scholars, such as Stephen Cohen (in [51]) who emphasises the discontinuities between Leninism and Stalinism. Cohen objects to their approval of certain developments in the 1930s which implies continuity between the radicalism of the early revolutionary years and the 1930s. They also offend the totalitarians since they find continuities between Leninism and Stalinism and the totalitarians lack sympathy for either. However, a critic of the 'new cohort' concedes that their emphasis on life at grass-roots and middle-management level tends to 'provide circumstantial evidence that some of the Stalinist policies were couched in terms which were not without their popular appeal, thus in effect raising the possibility that they were the product of shared perceptions and reasons rather than of Stalin's personal designs [33 *p. 40*].

To summarise: totalitarians emphasise the power of the state and the deliberate terrorisation of society. The state could and did crush any social group in its way and could even deliberately provoke a famine. Its goal was the atomisation of society. However, there were still areas where autonomy remained: one of these was the family (question: why will the state never be able to impose birth control? answer: because the means of production are in private hands!). Other examples are the persistence of religious faith, nationalism and ethnicity. Social historians have laboured to identify the social base of the Stalinist state, those who supported the regime and those who benefited from its policies. The main group consisted of the members of the party-state bureaucracies, the military, control agencies (NKVD and so on), mass organisations, party and *Komsomol* members. Fitzpatrick analyses the new élite [213], Kuromiya the younger generation of industrial workers [89], Viola workers promoting collectivisation [101], Siegelbaum the Stakhanovites [99]. What is striking about the social base so far identified is how narrow and insecure it was. Perhaps this was due, in part, to the tremendous social mobility and upheaval of the 1930s. On the other hand, there was considerable resistance at the work place and the labour process was slowed down. Studies of the immediate post-Stalin period reveal how ineffective controls were.

Totalitarians lay stress on state control of education, the mass media and propaganda in engendering social consent through mass indoctrination. This was probably more effective in the 1930s than later. Given the low level of education and lack of alternative sources of information, most Russians, at least, may have believed the official version. It is difficult to gauge the impact of ideological uniformity imposed by Stalin in 1933. People were afraid to express opposing views in public, but there was always the private sphere. Hence most citizens lived in two worlds, the official Soviet world and the private, real world. The language of discourse was determined by the state and one had to conform (for example, it was impossible to advocate the market as a solution to economic problems). The regime in the end was the loser as it refused to enter into a dialogue with the population. Social and personal responsibility declined. The educational system concentrated on narrow specialisation, and information on other disciplines was often in short supply. The long-term effect of this was catastrophic. Specialists failed to develop their capacity to analyse cause and effect and did not introduce the social dimension into their analysis. For instance, a doctor could not state that disease was the result of poor sanitation or malnutrition. Social historians tend to neglect the negative aspects of the above phenomena and instead insist upon the need to train new élites and modernise a backward country.

Totalitarians are on firmer ground when they underline the role of the state in mass mobilisation. The Soviet state lacked sophisticated institutions through which to channel social grievances. It used campaigns skilfully to put pressure on bureaucrats, factory managers and so on. These campaigns also identified potential recruits to the *apparat*. Social historians do not see mass mobilisation as something always directed from above. The local agenda often took over.

The Stalinist state was paradoxically very strong and very weak. Its weakness derived from the concentration of decision-making at the centre and the impact of forced collectivisation and industrialisation. The limited room for policy debates restricted the options available. Control mechanisms proliferated in the 1930s. The market economy's distributive and allocative functions had to be assumed by government, so the regime had to ensure the government did its job. This was a major task for the NKVD. It would appear that the attempt to proletarianise the state bureaucracy in 1936–38 was conceived of as a solution to the control problem by introducing a new generation of officials who were regarded as more politically reliable, untouched by previous political conflicts and with some industrial production experience. Totalitarians present a less sophisticated version of the above phenomena, seeing the state as strong and manipulative. Social historians, on the other hand, decline to conceptualise about the state.

Totalitarians see continuities between Leninism and Stalinism, emphasising the strong state, monopolistic communist party and the desire to transform society according to policy preferences at the top. Both Leninism and Stalinism are negative phenomena. The social historians are broadly in sympathy with the goals of Leninism and Stalinism and see links, but they are not necessarily negative. Sheila Fitzpatrick views the Russian revolution in a social context and concludes that it stretched from 1917 to the early 1930s.

Many of the hallmarks of Stalinism are constituent parts of Leninism: the strong state, the proletarianisation of the state, mass mobilisation, the elimination of capitalism from the economy, intolerance of opposing views, the use of terror as a policy instrument, death sentences for enemies of the state, instrumental relativism (the end justifies the means) and a low opinion of bureaucrats and the need to purge them from time to time. Lenin, and later Stalin, was confronted with the fundamental tension between revolutionary goals and the need to build up a strong Soviet state. This inevitably led to conflict over ideology and policy preferences as set goals were not achieved. Lenin and Stalin shared a common distrust of bureaucracy and never sought to bring into being a Weberian ideal type bureaucratic system. Instead, they preferred a revolutionary administrative system, components of which were mass mobilisation and class struggle. As the country moved towards socialism so the command-administrative system would be renewed, opposition would be eliminated and all negative phenomena eliminated. Hence Lenin and Stalin were both utopians. The state they were attempting to build was a utopian state and the ideology which was their fundamental inspiration a utopian ideology. Stalin caused greater pain and suffering and left a more flawed legacy because his experiment was on a truly epic scale.

However, there are also major dissimilarities between Lenin and Stalin. While Lenin was alive the revolution could be said to be following an essentially European course. The leading Bolsheviks, with the exception of Stalin, had all drunk deeply at the fountain of European culture. Many of them knew German and had read Marx in the original and were well versed in ideological controversies. Under Stalin there was a marked shift to an essentially Russian interpretation of socialism. Lenin had set in train the negation of the trend which had begun in 1861 with the emancipation of the serfs. Between 1861 and 1917 Russia had been moving towards European modes of political, economic and social life. The October Revolution cut the umbilical cord which linked Russia to the rest of Europe, but no one saw this at the time. Lenin did not think that revolution could survive unless there was a parallel revolution in at least some of the advanced industrial countries. Stalin, however, favoured practical and pragmatic administration, and the intellectual and theoretical approach to politics disappeared. Ministries and bureaux were no longer headed by men of stature whose standing was independent of the office they held; technicians took over whose main task was to achieve preordained goals. Hence Stalinism can be said to date from 1929 [51].

Stalin regarded himself as a 'creative' and not as a 'dogmatic' Marxist. In other words, he placed great emphasis on experience as a guide to action. Some commentators, Trotsky among them, would not accept that he had profound ideological convictions. They saw him as mainly concerned with manipulating Marxism–Leninism to suit his own ends. Some would even go so far as to claim that since he was not a believer himself, he did not expect anyone else to be a believer. He sought acquiescence. He propagated many myths to hide the appalling reality of the situation: that life was better and more joyous than before and improving all the time; that the Soviet Union was the most democratic country in the world; that power rested in the hands of the working class. Not only did Stalin know all this to be a fiction, the rest of the population did as well. It became part of the language of public discourse.

Yet believers were to be found [*Docs 28; 30*]. They were the yeast in the Soviet dough and were very zealous in the propagation of their faith. It is impossible to say how many there were. Belief in an omnipotent, omnipresent Stalin helped many people through the dark 1930s and lit up their hard lives. (However, no one refashioned the Lenin joke: Why are marriage beds always for three persons? Because Lenin is always with us!) Stalin expanded Marxist-Leninist thought. For example, he saw class struggle intensifying as the Soviet Union approached socialism.

Enormous attention was paid during the Stalin era to the correct formulation of Marxist–Leninist–Stalinist thought [*Doc. 23*]. It had to reflect experience because it was regarded as dynamic, just like life; hence, at any one time, it was very difficult to encapsulate it completely. One may view Stalin as taking ideology seriously since he hoped that the new *vir sovieticus*, Soviet man, and the new Soviet woman, *femina sovietica*, would emerge from the state-controlled environment. The goal was to develop personalities who, of their free will, would devote themselves to labour and to the service of the state. If the state could discover the 'objective scientific laws' of the language-conditioning process then success beckoned. However, these 'laws' were not discovered during Stalin's lifetime.

The Stalinist system was built on Leninist foundations. Lenin was a person of quite a different mould. Personally modest, a poor judge of men, uninterested in accumulating power for its own sake, keenly interested in intellectual debate and therefore in the views of others – providing they were progressive – he was genuinely concerned about the well-being of the working class. Lenin and Stalin shared a hatred of adulation at close quarters. Leninism meant first and foremost the rule of the party, albeit of its self-elected élite. Lenin always considered that the government, *Sovnarkom*, should run the country, with the Politburo as the final court of appeal. However, in practice, it was the party which filled key posts in the soviets, government, armed forces, *Cheka* and the trade unions. The party had accumulated great power, too much in Lenin's estimation, by the time of his death in 1924. Lenin, surprisingly, was often ill-informed about party affairs. He saw the danger Stalin's control of the 'machine' posed for the party and the state but was struck down before he could dismantle part of it. Bukharin, also, was aware of what was happening but was powerless to stop it. Lenin always objected to the term Leninism which appears to have surfaced by 1920. He regarded himself as a Marxist. Stalin developed the cult of personality and gradually took over as the fount of wisdom from the party. Great deeds were done in his name. Yet oddly enough no attempt was made to integrate the role of the individual into Marxist–Leninist–Stalinist thought during Stalin's years. Stalinism was the negation of Lenin's nationality policy. Lenin, in his 'Testament', called the Georgian a 'Great Russian chauvinist' and perceived for the first time how far their views on nationality diverged. Lenin wanted the non-Russian nationalities to stay in the Soviet Union by choice. Stalin wanted to mould them according to Russian norms. The concept of the non-Russian as the younger brother and the Russian as the elder brother is revealing.

Given the shortcomings of the totalitarians (the intentionalists) and the social historians (the structuralists), it is worth attempting a more rounded approach which pays due attention to the interaction of political and social policies. Following Tucker [50], this can be called the reconstruction–consolidation or 'reccon' approach. This views the history of the Soviet Union as a series of advances and retreats in order to consolidate gains. Revolution and war communism was an advance; NEP was a retreat in order to allow the Bolsheviks to build up their strength before attempting further advance; 1928–32 was a whirlwind advance; 1933–36 was a temporary slowdown to consolidate; 1937–39 was another violent advance; 1939–41 was less radical with the ending of the purges; then war intervened; 1946–52 again saw consolidation; but in 1952–53 it would appear that Stalin was considering another assault on the bureaucracy and party. The evidence for this was the smaller and larger Presidium elected at the XIXth Party Congress and the 'doctors' plot'.

The reccon approach gives due weight to the power of the state but also takes into account social resistance to official policy. This explains the need for periods of consolidation. The crisis of 1932–33, the terrible famine and the slowdown in growth rates, all of which put Stalin's position in jeopardy, made necessary the period of consolidation which followed. Recent research has revealed that Stalin and Molotov were convinced that there was widespread opposition to the regime in the 1930s which could become critically important in the event of war. This may explain the assault on the Red Army in 1937–38. In addition, Molotov and Kaganovich had their doubts about the wisdom of aspects of the violent advance of 1937–39 which included the wiping out of the Old Bolsheviks. The advances built on previous experience. The 1936–38 purges are inconceivable without the accumulated experience of war communism and 1928–32. The terror can be seen as evidence of the weakness of the regime as it struck out against perceived enemies. The terror redefined societal relations and promoted social mobility. Egalitarianism was pushed aside by the late 1930s. There are also parallels between the USSR and China. After the Great Leap Forward came a period of calm, followed by the Cultural Revolution. Mao was always concerned to proletarianise the bureaucracy and downgrade accumulated expertise.

Trotsky's interpretation of Stalin had been influential. As a Marxist he was concerned to provide a Marxist critique of the Stalinist phenomenon. This downgraded the role of the individual and placed great emphasis on circumstances. Trotsky came up with concepts of 'Thermidorian reaction' and 'bureaucratic degeneration'. On Thermidor 9 (27 July 1794) Robespierre and other Jacobin leaders were overthrown and the French revolution glided into reaction. Whereas the French Thermidor happened quickly, the Soviet Thermidor took its time. The failure of socialist revolution abroad led to the gradual degeneration of the revolution at home. Russia's minuscule working class, decimated, dispersed and weakened by war, revolution and famine, could not elevate the gains of October to a fully functioning democratic dictatorship of the proletariat. Instead, a bureaucratic Leviathan, the totalitarian party-state machine, placed itself above society and took control of politics, administration and the manufacture and distribution of scarce goods. Russia's fledgeling civil society was overwhelmed as commissars, enterprise managers, party functionaries, soviet officials – *apparatchiki* who controlled supply and distribution of goods and services – took control of the small 'surplus product'. They were little concerned about the ideals of October. Stalin was *apparat* man personified. Initially the *apparat* sided with the right, since only the conditions of NEP could guarantee its privileges. Stalin was forced into a violent struggle with the 'revolutionary vanguard', the left and United Opposition. After their defeat the contradictions of NEP obliged Stalin to turn on the right and introduce the 'third phase' of Soviet history, collectivisation and industrialisation, orchestrated from above. To Trotsky, the decay of socialism was not the fault of Lenin or the Bolshevik party or the left or the United Opposition. It was due to the coming together of a unique set of historical circumstances. The 'dialectics of history' had thrown up Stalin who worked through human instruments fashioned by NEP, the dross, the flotsam, the bureaucrats, the sneaks, the 'worms who were crawling out of the upturned soil of the manured revolution' [57 *p. 31*]. Trotsky was convinced that Stalinism could not last. In the end he was right but he did not live to see its demise.

Deutscher, as a supporter of Trotsky, broadly accepts this picture [23]. Stalin, to him, was not a great man or even one approaching greatness, but very ordinary. It was the machine which made and kept him in power. Stalin was not inevitable, others could have piloted the Soviet ship towards socialism.

E.H. Carr sees Stalin as an average political leader borne along by the dynamic forces of the revolution [1]. Industrialisation was inevitable; therefore someone would have directed the revolution to its natural conclusion. It just happened that Stalin, the 'wonderful Georgian', in Lenin's term, was the person to do so. Carr credits Stalin with greater ability than Trotsky, but he still sees him as someone moulded by the times rather than moulding the times. The excesses associated with the cult of personality were unfortunate but they were not strong enough to negate the dynamic forces which were propelling the Russian revolution forward. Carr comes close to stating that Stalinism happened because it had to happen. Therefore, contesting visions of socialism are irrelevant. Moral judgement and discussion about alternative routes to socialism are idle speculation [33].

Roy Medvedev is a determined critic of Stalinism [6; 7]. He is an ardent Leninist and believes that Stalinism amounts to nothing more than pseudosocialism. Stalin, in his view, corrupted and distorted Lenin's noble vision of the Soviet Union. Aleksandr Solzhenitsyn does not accept that Stalinism ever existed since Stalin was merely the 'blind, mechanical executor' of Lenin's will. He also has a low opinion of Lenin.

Stalinism in the full-blown sense only came into being after 1936. Hence it is necessary to bear in mind that this phenomenon evolved over time and is therefore different during the various stages of its growth. One can speak of various degrees of Stalinism. Whether one approves or disapproves of it, it was a truly remarkable phenomenon, one that profoundly marked the twentieth century. One can only approve of it if one suspends moral judgement.

PART FOUR: DOCUMENTS

DOCUMENT 1 **THE PARTY**

Stalin here spells out systematically his understanding of the role of the Communist Party. This document was originally published in 1924 and is one of the foundation stones of Leninism which Stalin, more than anyone else, developed.

What are the specific features of this new party?

1. *The Party as the vanguard of the working class.* The Party must be, first of all, the *vanguard* of the working class. The Party must absorb all the best elements of the working class, their experience, their revolutionary spirit, their selfless devotion to the cause of the proletariat. But in order that it may really be the vanguard, the Party must be armed with revolutionary theory, with a knowledge of the laws of the movement, with a knowledge of the laws of revolution. Without this it will be incapable of directing the struggle of the proletariat, of leading the proletariat. The Party cannot be a real party if it limits itself to registering what the masses of the working class feel and think, if it drags at the tail of the spontaneous movement, if it is unable to overcome the inertness and the political indifference of the spontaneous movement, if it is unable to rise above the momentary interests of the proletariat, if it is unable to elevate the masses to the level of the class interests of the proletariat. The Party must stand at the head of the working class; it must see farther than the working class; it must lead the proletariat, and not follow in the tail of the spontaneous movement. ...

No army at war can dispense with an experienced General Staff if it does not want to court certain defeat. Is it not clear that the proletariat can still less dispense with such a General Staff if it does not want to give itself up to be devoured by its mortal enemies? But where is this General Staff? Only the revolutionary party of the proletariat can serve as this General Staff. The working class without a revolutionary party is an army without a General Staff. The Party is the General Staff of the proletariat. ...

2. *The Party as the organized detachment of the working class.* The Party is not only the vanguard detachment of the working class. If it desires really to direct the struggle of the class it must at the same time be the organized

detachment of its class.

3. *The Party as the highest form of class organization of the proletariat.*
The Party is the organized detachment of the working class.

This organization is the Party of the proletariat. ... the Party, as the best
school for training leaders of the working class, is, by reason of its
experience and prestige, the only organization capable of centralizing the
leadership of the struggle of the proletariat, thus transforming each and
every non-Party organization of the working class into an auxiliary body
and transmission belt linking the Party with the class. The Party is the
highest form of class organization of the proletariat. ...

4. *The Party as the instrument of the dictatorship of the proletariat.* ... The
Party is not only the highest form of class association of the proletarians; it
is at the same an *instrument* in the hands of the proletariat *for* achieving the
dictatorship where that has not yet been achieved and *for* consolidating and
expanding the dictatorship where it has already been achieved. ...

The proletariat needs the Party *for* the purpose of achieving and
maintaining the dictatorship. The Party is an instrument of the dictatorship
of the proletariat.

5. *The Party as the embodiment of unity of will, incompatible with the
existence of factions.* The achievement and maintenance of the dictatorship
of the proletariat is impossible without a party which is strong by reason of
its solidarity and iron discipline. ... Iron discipline does not preclude but
presupposes conscious and voluntary submission, for only conscious
discipline can be truly iron discipline. But after a contest of opinion has
been closed, after criticism has been exhausted and a decision has been
arrived at, unity of will and unity of action of all Party members are the
necessary conditions without which neither Party unity nor iron discipline in
the Party is conceivable. ...

But from this it follows that the existence of factions is incompatible
either with the Party's unity or with its iron discipline.

6. *The Party is strengthened by purging itself of opportunist elements.*
The source of factionalism in the Party is its opportunist elements. ... Our
Party succeeded in creating internal unity and unexampled cohesion of its
ranks primarily because it was able in good time to purge itself of the
opportunist pollution, because it was able to rid its ranks of the
Liquidators, the Mensheviks. Proletarian parties develop and become strong
by purging themselves of opportunists and reformists, social-imperialists and
social-chauvinists, social-patriots, and social-pacifists. The Party becomes
strong by purging itself of opportunist elements.

J. Stalin [47], pp. 97–109.

DOCUMENT 2   THE RIGHT DEVIATION

Published in April 1929, this condemnation of Bukharin and his supporters is a good example of Stalin's political style. Note how he blackens the Right by asserting that support for them means betrayal of the revolution. By 1929 he was in a position to decide what was in the best interests of the revolution.

The fight against the Right deviation is one of the most decisive duties of our party. If we, in our own ranks, in our own party, in the political General Staff of the proletariat, which is directing the movement and is leading the proletariat forward – if we in this General Staff tolerated the free existence and the free functioning of the Right deviationists, who are trying to demobilize the party, to demoralize the working class, to adapt our policy to the tastes of the 'Soviet' bourgeoisie, and thus yield to the difficulties of our construction – if we tolerated all this, what would it mean? Would it not mean that we want to send the revolution down hill, demoralize our socialist construction, flee from difficulties, surrender our positions to the capitalist elements? Does Bukharin's group understand that to refuse to fight the Right deviation is to *betray* the working class, to *betray* the revolution?

J. Stalin [47], pp. 371–2.

DOCUMENT 3   DIZZY WITH SUCCESS

This is part of an article which appeared in Pravda *on 2 March 1930. Collectivisation was supposed to be voluntary but officials herded peasants into collectives against their will. To reduce the mayhem in the countryside and to ensure that the spring sowing was done, Stalin called a temporary halt. It was only tactical, as collectivisation was stepped up later in the year.*

But what really happens sometimes? Can it be said that the voluntary principle and the principle of allowing for local peculiarities are not violated in a number of districts? No, unfortunately, that cannot be said. We know, for example, that in a number of the Northern districts of the grain-importing belt, where there are comparatively fewer favourable conditions for the immediate organization of collective farms than in the grain-growing districts, not infrequently efforts are made to *substitute* for preparatory work in organizing collective farms the bureaucratic decreeing of a collective farm movement from above, paper resolutions on the growth of collective farms, the formulation of collective farms on paper – of farms which do not yet exist, but regarding the 'existence' of which there is a pile of boastful resolutions. Or, take certain districts in Turkestan, where there are even fewer favourable conditions for the immediate organization of collective farms than in the Northern regions of the grain-importing belt. We know that in a number of districts in Turkestan attempts have already been made to 'overtake and outstrip' the advanced districts of the U.S.S.R. by the method of threatening to resort to military force, by the method of threatening to deprive the peasants who do not as yet want to join the collective farms of irrigation water and of manufactured goods.

What is there in common between this Sergeant Prishibeyev 'policy' and the party's policy which rests on the voluntary principle and allows for local peculiarities in collective farm construction? Obviously, they have not, nor can they have, anything in common.

J. Stalin [47], pp. 421–2.

DOCUMENT 4   **THE BREAKNECK SPEED OF INDUSTRIALISATION**

Those who favoured a slowdown in industrialisation were answered by Stalin in 1931. He had a long memory for past Russian defeats, something one would not have expected of a Soviet leader. Note that past German defeats have been omitted.

It is sometimes asked whether it is not possible to slow down the tempo a bit, to put a check on the movement. No, comrades, it is not possible! The tempo must not be reduced! On the contrary, we must increase it as much as is within our powers and possibilities. This is dictated to us by our obligations to the workers and peasants of the U.S.S.R. This is dictated to us by our obligations to the working class of the whole world.

To slacken the tempo would mean falling behind. And those who fall behind get beaten. But we do not want to be beaten. No, we refuse to be beaten! One feature of the history of old Russia was the continual beatings she suffered for falling behind, for her backwardness. She was beaten by the Mongol Khans. She was beaten by the Turkish beys. She was beaten by the Swedish feudal lords. She was beaten by the Polish and Lithuanian gentry. She was beaten by the British and French capitalists. She was beaten by the Japanese barons. All beat her – for her backwardness: for military backwardness, for cultural backwardness, for political backwardness, for industrial backwardness, for agricultural backwardness. She was beaten because to do so was profitable and could be done with impunity. Do you remember the words of the pre-revolutionary poet: 'You are poor and abundant, mighty and impotent, Mother Russia.' These words of the old poet were well learned by those gentlemen. They beat her, saying: 'You are abundant,' so one can enrich oneself at your expense. They beat her, saying: 'You are poor and impotent,' so you can be beaten and plundered with impunity. Such is the law of the exploiters – to beat the backward and the weak. It is the jungle law of capitalism. You are backward, you are weak – therefore you are wrong; hence, you can be beaten and enslaved. You are mighty – therefore you are right; hence, we must be wary of you.

That is why we must no longer lag behind.

In the past we had no fatherland, nor could we have one. But now that we have overthrown capitalism and power is in the hands of the working class, we have a fatherland, and we will defend its independence. Do you want our socialist fatherland to be beaten and to lose its independence? If you do not want this you must put an end to its backwardness in the shortest possible time and develop genuine Bolshevik tempo in building up its socialist system of economy. There is no other way. That is why Lenin said during the October Revolution: 'Either perish, or overtake and outstrip the advanced capitalist countries.'

We are fifty or a hundred years behind the advanced countries. We must make good this distance in ten years. Either we do it, or they crush us.

J. Stalin [47], pp. 455–6.

DOCUMENT 5   **AN END TO SPECIALIST-BAITING**

During the first years of the first Five-Year Plan 'bourgeois' or non-communist specialists had been subjected to abuse and harassment. Many were arrested and some lost their lives. The goal was to do away with any independence they had vis-à-vis the state. On 23 June 1931 Stalin decided that they were no longer a threat.

But it follows from this that we must change our policy towards the old technical intelligentsia accordingly. Whereas during the height of the wrecking activities our attitude towards the old technical intelligentsia was mainly expressed by the policy of routing them, now, when these intellectuals are turning to the side of the Soviet government, our attitude towards them must be expressed mainly in the policy of enlisting them and solicitude for them. It would be wrong and undialectical to continue our former policy under the new, changed conditions. It would be stupid and unwise to regard practically every expert and engineer of the old school as an undetected criminal and wrecker. We have always regarded and still regard 'expert-baiting' as a harmful and disgraceful phenomenon.

Hence, the task is *to change our attitude towards the engineers and technicians of the old school, to show them greater attention and solicitude, to display more boldness in enlisting their co-operation.*

J. Stalin [47], pp. 475–6.

DOCUMENT 6   WAGE DIFFERENTIALS REINTRODUCED

The egalitarianism of the early years of industrialisation did not produce the growth in labour productivity expected. In June 1931 Stalin therefore reverted to the old system.

What is the cause of the heavy turnover of labour power?

The cause is the wrong structure of wages, the wrong wage scales, the 'Leftist' practice of wage equalization. In a number of our factories wage scales are drawn up in such a way as to practically wipe out the difference between skilled labor and unskilled labor, between heavy work and light work. The consequence of wage equalization is that the unskilled worker lacks the incentive to become a skilled worker and is thus deprived of the prospect of advancement; as a result he feels himself a 'sojourner' in the factory, working only temporarily so as to earn a little and then go off to 'seek his fortune' elsewhere. The consequence of wage equalization is that the skilled worker is obliged to wander from factory to factory until he finds one where his skill is properly appreciated.

Hence the 'general' drift from factory to factory; hence the heavy turnover of labor power.

In order to put an end to this evil we must abolish wage equalization and discard the old wage scales. In order to put an end to this evil we must draw up wage scales that will take into account the difference between skilled labor and unskilled labor, between heavy work and light work.

J. Stalin [47], p. 463.

DOCUMENT 7   FULFILMENT OF THE PRINCIPAL GOALS OF THE STALINIST FIVE YEAR PLANS 1928–50

The following table estimates to what extent the principal goals of the Five-Year Plans were achieved. Jasny, Bergson, Nutter, Kaplan, Moorsteen, Johnson and Kahan are western economists. Figures are given in percentages.

	First Five-Year Plan (1928–1932) (1)	Second Five-Year Plan (1933–1937) (2)	Fourth Five-Year Plan (1946–1950) (3)
National Income			
1. Official Soviet estimate (1926/27 prices)	91.5	96.1	118.9
2. Jasny estimate (1926/27 'real' prices)	70.2	66.5	
3. Bergson estimate			89.9
4. Nutter estimate			84.1

	First Five-Year Plan (1928–1932) (1)	Second Five-Year Plan (1933–1937) (2)	Fourth Five-Year Plan (1946–1950) (3)
Industrial Production			
5. Official Soviet estimate (1926/27 prices)	100.7	103.0	116.9
6. Jasny estimate	69.9	81.2	
7. Nutter estimate	59.7	93.1	83.8
8. Kaplan and Moorsteen estimate	65.3	75.7	94.9
9. Official Soviet estimate, producer goods (1926/27 prices)	127.6	121.3	127.5
10. Official Soviet estimate, consumer goods (1926/27 prices)	80.5	85.4	95.7
Agricultural Production			
11. Official Soviet estimates (1926/27 prices)	57.8	62.6–76.9	89.9
12. Jasny estimate	49.6	76.7	
13. Nutter estimate	50.7	69.0	76.4
14. Johnson and Kahan estimates	52.4	66.1–69.0	79.4
Transport			
15. Railway freight traffic (ton–km)	104.0		113.2
Employment			
16. National economy, workers and employees	144.9	93.4	116.1
17. Industry, workers and employees	173.9		118.9
Wages (workers and employees, nat. economy)			
18. Average money wage	143.9	173.6	127.8
19. Average real wage, official Soviet estimate	31.9	102.6	89.1
20. Average real wage, Zaleski estimate	26.0	65.8	
Labor Productivity, Industry			
21. Official Soviet estimate	65.1		100.7
22. Jasny estimate	41.8		
23. Nutter estimate	36.3		
24. Kaplan and Moorsteen estimate			80.0
Cost of Production			
25. Industry (current prices)	146.1	121.2	134.2
Investment			
26. In constant prices	54.0		122.0

E. Zaleski [105], p. 503.

Note: Khanin [81] estimates industrial growth over the years 1928–41 at 10.9 per cent annually (officially 17 per cent) and national income growth at 3.2 per cent (officially 13.9 per cent).

DOCUMENT 8   MANDELSTAM'S POEM ABOUT STALIN
(NOVEMBER 1933)

Osip Mandelstam was arrested in May 1934 for composing this poem,
which he had recited at a gathering. Stalin got to know about it and was
offended by the unflattering reference to him. This was enough to lead to
Mandelstam's arrest and eventual death in a labour camp.

We live, deaf to the land beneath us,
Ten steps away no one hears our speeches,

But where there's so much as half a conversation
The Kremlin's mountaineer will get his mention.[1]

His fingers are fat as grubs
And the words, final as lead weights, fall from his lips,

His cockroach whiskers leer
And his boot tops gleam.

Around him a rabble of thin-necked leaders –
fawning half-men for him to play with.

They whinny, purr or whine
As he prates and points a finger,

One by one forging his laws, to be flung
Like horseshoes at the head, the eye or the groin.

And every killing is a treat
For the broad-chested Ossete.[2]

[1] In the first version, which came into the hands of the secret police, these two lines
read:

All we hear is the Kremlin mountaineer,
The murderer and peasant-slayer.

[2] 'Ossete'. There were persistent stories that Stalin had Ossetian blood. Ossetia is to
the north of Georgia in the Caucasus. The people, of Iranian stock, are quite different
from the Georgians.

N. Mandelstam [37], p. 13.

DOCUMENT 9   (a) INTERROGATION TECHNIQUES

Osip Mandelstam (M. in the text) was subjected to various types of treatment, here described by Nadezhda Mandelstam, his wife. The police could always rely on a steady flow of denunciations. It was one way of exacting revenge for past wrongs. Informers were everywhere as well.

At the very first interrogation M. had admitted to being the author of the poem on Stalin, so the stool pigeon's task could not have been merely to find out something that M. was hiding. Part of the function of these people was to unnerve and wear down prisoners under interrogation, to make their lives a misery. Until 1937 our secret police made much of their psychological methods, but afterward these gave way to physical torture, with beatings of the most primitive kind. After 1937 I never again heard of anyone being held in solitary confinement cells, with or without stool pigeons. Perhaps people picked out for such treatment after 1937 did not leave the Lubianka alive. M. was put through the physical ordeal which had always been applied. It consisted mainly of not being allowed to sleep. He was called out every night and kept for hours on end. Most of the time was spent not in actual questioning, but in waiting under guard outside the interrogator's door. Once, when there was no interrogation, he was wakened all the same and taken to see a woman who kept him waiting at the door of her office for many hours, only to ask him at the end of it whether he had any complaints. Everybody knew how meaningless it was to make complaints to the prosecutor, and M. did not avail himself of this right. He had probably been called to her office simply as a formality, and also to keep him awake even on a night when the interrogator was catching up on his own sleep. These night birds lived a preposterous life, but all the same they managed to get some sleep, although not at the times when ordinary mortals did. The ordeal by deprivation of sleep and a bright light shining right in the eyes are known to everybody who has gone through such interrogations.

The work of undermining a person's sanity was carried on quite systematically in the Lubianka, and since our secret police is a bureaucratic institution like any other, all the procedures involved were probably governed by precise instructions. Even though the personnel were specifically selected for the job, one cannot ascribe what went on to their wicked nature, since the same people could overnight have become kindness itself – if so instructed. There were rumours among us that Yagoda had set up secret laboratories and staffed them with specialists who were carrying out all kinds of experiments with drugs, hypnosis, phonograph records and so forth. It was impossible to check such stories, and they may have been a product of our morbid imaginations, or tales deliberately put about to keep us all on tenterhooks.

The interrogator's arrogance was reflected not only in his manner, but also in occasional very superior remarks that smacked of the literary drawing room. The first generation of young Chekists, later to be removed and destroyed in 1937, was distinguished by its sophisticated tastes and weakness for literature – only the most fashionable, of course. In my presence Christophorovich said to M. that it was useful for a poet to experience fear ('you yourself told me so') because it can inspire verse, and that he would 'experience fear in full measure.' Both M. and I noted the use of the future tense. In what Moscow drawing rooms had Christophorovich heard this kind of talk?

Apart from people who were forced into cooperating, there were hosts of volunteers. Denunciations poured into every institution on a quite unmanageable scale. Before the Twentieth Congress [1956] I heard an inspector of the Ministry of Education address a meeting at the Chuvash Teachers' Training College, where I was then working, and ask the staff to stop writing denunciations, warning them that anonymous ones would no longer be read at all. Can it be true that they no longer read anonymous denunciations? I find it hard to believe.

Because of this system of 'interviews', people developed two kinds of phobia – some suspected that everybody they met was an informer, others that they might be taken for one.

One final question: was it my fault for not getting rid of all our friends and acquaintances, as did most good wives and mothers at that time? My guilt is lessened only by the fact that M. would in any case have given me the slip and found a way of reading his outrageous poem – and in this country all real poetry is outrageous – to the first person he met. He was not one to put a gag on himself and lead a life of voluntary seclusion.

N. Mandelstam [37], pp. 75–6.

DOCUMENT 9   (b) AUNT LESIA

This report is by Chrystia Freeland, a Canadian journalist, describing the arrest and travail of her favourite great-aunt, Oleksandra Blavatska, or Aunt Lesia.

My favourite great-aunt spent 10 years in Stalinist labour camps for two crimes: buying a funeral wreath and playing the harp at a dinner party. The funeral wreath was purchased in 1944 when Aunt Lesia was 19 years old. ... It was for Metropolitan Sheptytsky, head of the Ukrainian Catholic Church. He was revered ... 'as the holiest of holies' for his defiance of both the Nazis and the Soviets during the Second World War. ... 'We bought a beautiful wreath with red linden at the centre, as was the Ukrainian custom.... And on a black band draped across the wreath we wrote: "To the unforgettable defender of Ukrainian youth, from the students of the Soviet Trade Institute." The Bolsheviks – not known for their sense of humour – could never forgive me for that.'

The day after the funeral she was expelled from the Institute and the midnight interrogations at KGB headquarters, which began for Lesia as soon as the Red Army took over the western Ukrainian city of Lviv, intensified. But a dinner party a few months later was the last straw. When a delegation of Soviet Ukrainian writers came to Lviv they were entertained by Lesia's mother, the city's most accomplished hostess in the old days of the Austro-Hungarian, and later Polish, rule. While Mrs Blavatska charmed the writers by chatting in French, her daughter, the only harpist in the city (the harp was a ploy to get Lesia into the Conservatory after she had been expelled from the Trade Institute) provided a musical accomplishment.

A few weeks later, Lesia was arrested on her way to the Conservatory and she began an education of a different sort. Over the next decade she progressed from KGB interrogation cells to a tour of Soviet labour camps. Along the way, she gave birth to my second favourite aunt Vira, 'Faith', who spent her early childhood separated from her mother in a Soviet orphanage.

'The KGB cell had an open window and it was winter, so there was ice and snow on the floor. It was full of rats. It was exactly seven steps wide: I know because I paced back and forth all day and all night.' After 18 days in the isolation cell, Lesia collapsed. 'I was young and I loved to dance but I told myself that if I was ever again able to walk I would never dance. I've kept that promise.' Unconscious, Lesia was carried into a larger, crowded jail cell, where she spent two months, and then she was sentenced. 'Because I was so young and they really couldn't find anything at all to accuse me of I was given what we called a child's sentence, just 10 years of hard labour and five years of exile in Siberia.' The journeys between the camps were the worst part. 'A hundred prisoners would be herded into locked cattle cars with a hole in the middle to act as a toilet. Every day we were given one slice of salted herring, a piece of bread and a bottle of water. ... I couldn't bring myself to eat the herring and maybe that was what saved me.'

Early in her sentence, when she was in a labour camp in Estonia, Lesia was conned by more savvy inmates into selling part of her food ration in exchange for promised assistance to escape. 'That was, of course, very stupid, because no one ever escaped Stalin's camps. But I was tricked and I sold them some of my food. My body began to decay and one day the work captain said he would no longer accept me, so I got even less food. Slowly, I began to die.' Saved by a sympathetic doctor in the prison infirmary, Lesia recovered and was sent to the labour camp in Mordova, in north-western Russia, where she would serve most of her sentence. Vira, born in the Estonia prison, was initially kept together with other children in a camp adjacent to her mother's but when the children were 18 months old they were sent to an orphanage in Siberia. 'If the caretaker at the orphanage was very kind, once a year she would send me a letter about my daughter. Three times the prison warders called me and asked me to give her up for adoption, but each time I refused and began a hunger strike. Eventually they gave up,' While Vira grew up, her mother devoted herself to survival. 'It was a very select camp: we had the prima ballerina of the Minsk ballet, Hitler's private secretary, a few Parisians and some Moscow girls who had married diplomats.' ... Lesia preserved her body with a rapidly acquired public cunning ... and her soul with small acts of private defiance. She proudly shows me the relic of one such gesture: a misshapen gold wedding band, her mother's, which Lesia hid from the prison warders during a decade of body searches by wearing it under a dirt encrusted bandage on one of her toes. 'For 10 years I didn't take that bandage off. It was so dirty and disgusting and rotten it made my skin crawl to look at it. But the guards couldn't bear to examine it too closely either, so I still have my mother's wedding ring. I think I might be one of the only people who ever managed to hide something from Stalin's police.' ...

One last question: how did you survive? 'I'm not sure. We former political prisoners often tell each other that the experience has warped us all somehow. That's probably true, but I think I still appear to be quite normal. Maybe it was because my mother was such a strong disciplinarian and always insisted on good manners. Even in the labour camps, I never learned to swear, although many did; I never learned to smoke, although many did; and unlike the more cosmopolitan girls from the big cities, I never became a lesbian.'

Financial Times (London), 13–14 August 1994.

DOCUMENT 10   **LIFE BEFORE THE PURGES**

Nadezhda Mandelstam describes the atmosphere of the mid-1930s, before the terror became more devastating in 1937.

In the years of the 'breathing-space', before the terror began in earnest, there were always fairly widespread arrests, particularly among the intelligentsia, in the spring (mostly in May) and in the fall. They were meant to distract attention from our perennial economic failures. At that time there were scarcely any cases of people disappearing into thin air: they always wrote from exile, and returned at the end of their sentences – to be deported again. Andrei Bely, when we met him at Koktebel in the summer of 1933, said he could scarcely keep up with the business of sending telegrams and writing letters to all his friends who had just 'returned' – there had evidently been a clean sweep of theosophists, who were then released all at the same time in 1933. Similarly, in the spring before M.'s arrest, Piast had returned. After three or five years' absence all such exiles came back and were allowed to settle in small towns beyond a hundred kilometres from Moscow.

N. Mandelstam [37], p. 12.

DOCUMENT 11   THE EFFECTS OF THE PURGES

By the middle of May 1937 the line at the MGB window had dwindled to a
dozen or so gloomy and shabbily dressed intellectuals. 'Everybody's left
Voronezh', M. whispered to me. Despite our isolation, we at once
understood the reason: nearly all the old exiles had been re-arrested and no
new ones were being sent. The 'vegetarian' phase was over. People were no
longer being banished, as we had been. From prison one now went either to
a forced-labor camp or to the other world. A privileged few were kept in
prison. The wives and children of prisoners were no longer sent into
enforced residence away from the big cities, but were now also interned in
special camps. There were even special institutions for small children, who
were seen as potential avengers for their fathers.

N. Mandelstam [37], p. 212.

DOCUMENT 12   THE RATIONALE BEHIND THE MASS
               TERROR

The principles and aims of mass terror have nothing in common with
ordinary police work or with security. The only purpose of terror is
intimidation. To plunge the whole country into a state of chronic fear, the
number of victims must be raised to astronomical levels, and on every floor
of every building there must always be several apartments from which the
tenants have suddenly been taken away. The remaining inhabitants will be
model citizens for the rest of their lives – this will be true for every street
and every city through which the broom has swept. The only essential thing
for those who rule by terror is not to overlook the new generations growing
up without faith in their elders, and to keep on repeating the process in
systematic fashion. Stalin ruled for a long time and saw to it that the waves
of terror recurred from time to time, always on an even greater scale than
before.

N. Mandelstam [37], pp. 316–17.

DOCUMENT 13   (a) STALIN AND THE PURGES

*This is a typical document forwarded by Ezhov to Stalin during the Purges.
On 30 July 1937 Stalin, Molotov and Kaganovich learned that a total of
258,950 persons were included in categories 1 and 2 and hence were to be
executed. This order was then sent to the republics,* krais *and* oblasts. *It*

*was up to the local NKVD organs to lay their hands on these 'enemies of
the people.' Often they made counter-proposals and exceeded the norm for
their region. In August 1937 Ezhov asked Stalin to sanction the persecution
of persons of Polish nationality.*

*On the document is: Agreed. J. Stalin, V. Molotov, L. Kaganovich,
S. Kossior. As a result, between August and December 1937 a total of
18,193 Poles were executed or arrested.*

Order no. 00447

To comrade Stalin,

I am forwarding you for confirmation four lists of persons who come within
the jurisdiction of the military collegium:

1.   List no. 1 (general)
2.   List no. 2 (ex-military)
3.   List no. 3 (ex-NKVD employees)
4.   List no. 4 (wives of enemies of the people)

I request permission to condemn all to the category 1 sentence.

Signed: Ezhov

[The lists were checked by Stalin and Molotov. On each list is the remark: Agreed.
J. Stalin, V. Molotov.]

Jahrbuch [109], p. 234.

(b)

*From the late 1940s Stalin personally reviewed all charges against persons
of Jewish nationality.*

3 April 1952

To comrade Stalin,

I enclose a copy of the indictment against the Jewish nationalists and
American spies Lozowsky, Fefer and others. I report that the investigation
report has been forwarded to the military collegium of the USSR Supreme
Court for review with the recommendation that Lozowsky, Fefer and all the
other accused, with the exception of Stern, be executed by shooting. Stern
should be banned to a far away part of the country for 10 years.

Signed: S. Ignatev, USSR Minister for State Security

[Stalin agreed to this request but reduced Stern's banishment to 5 years.]

Jahrbuch [109], p. 233.

DOCUMENT 14 THE IMPACT OF THE TERROR ON EVERYDAY LIVES

As regards the Stalinist terror, we always knew that it might wax or wane, but that it might end – this we could never imagine. What reason was there for it to end? Everybody seemed intent on his daily round and went smiling about the business of carrying out his instructions. It was essential to smile – if you didn't, it meant you were afraid or discontented. This nobody could affort to admit – if you were afraid, then you must have a bad conscience. Everybody who worked for the State – and in this country even the humblest stall-keeper is a bureaucrat – had to strut around wearing a cheerful expression, as though to say: 'What's going on is no concern of mine, I have very important work to do, and I'm terribly busy. I am trying to do my best for the State, so do not get in my way. My conscience is clear – if what's-his-name has been arrested, there must be good reason.' The mask was taken off only at home, and then not always – even from your children you had to conceal how horror-struck you were; otherwise, God save you, they might let something slip in school. ... Some people had adapted to the terror so well that they knew how to profit from it – there was nothing out of the ordinary about denouncing a neighbour to get his apartment or his job. But while wearing your smiling mask, it was important not to laugh – this could look suspicious to the neighbours and make them think you were indulging in sacrilegious mockery.

N. Mandelstam [37], pp. 304–5.

DOCUMENT 15 THE COMING INTO BEING OF A NEW ÉLITE

At the end of the twenties and in the thirties our authorities, making no concession to 'egalitarianism', started to raise the living standard of those who had proved their usefulness. The resulting differentiation was very noticeable, and everybody was concerned to keep the material benefits he had worked so hard to earn – particularly now that the wretched poverty of the first post-revolutionary years was a thing of the past. Nobody wanted to go through that again, and a thin layer of privileged people gradually came into being – with 'packets', country villas, and cars. They realized only later how precarious it all was: in the period of the great purges they found they could be stripped of everything in a flash, and without any explanation. But in the meantime those who had been granted a share of the cake eagerly did everything demanded of them.

N. Mandelstam [37], p. 231.

DOCUMENT 16   STALIN CARES ABOUT PEOPLE

Stalin was concerned to project himself as father of the people: someone who cared about everyone. In reality he placed material goals first and people second.

I recall an incident in Siberia, where I lived at one time in exile. It was in the spring, at the time of the spring floods. About thirty men went to the river to pull out timber which had been carried away by the vast, swollen river. Towards evening they returned to the village, but with one comrade missing. When asked where the thirtieth man was, they replied indifferently that the thirtieth man had 'remained there'. To my question, 'How do you mean, remained there?' they replied with the same indifference, 'Why ask – drowned, of course'. And thereupon one of them began to hurry away, saying, 'I've got to go and water the mare'. When I reproached them with having more concern for animals than for men, one of them said, amid the general approval of the rest: 'Why should we be concerned about men? We can always make men. But a mare ... just try and make a mare.' Here you have a case, not very significant perhaps, but very characteristic. It seems to me that the indifference of certain of our leaders to people, to cadres, their inability to value people, is a survival of that strange attitude of man to man displayed in the episode in far-off Siberia that I have just related.

J. Stalin [47], pp. 661–2.

DOCUMENT 17   STALIN THE MIRACLE-WORKER

Bukharin acted as the protector of the literary élite as long as he was at liberty. His intervention on Mandelstam's behalf reveals that Stalin's word was absolute.

In his letter to Stalin, Bukharin added a postscript saying he had been visited by [Boris] Pasternak, who was upset by the arrest of Mandelstam. The purpose of this postscript was clear: it was Bukharin's way of indicating to Stalin what the effect of M.'s arrest had been on public opinion. It was always necessary to personify 'public opinion' in this way.

You were allowed to talk of one particular individual being upset, but it was unthinkable to mention the existence of dissatisfaction among a whole section of the community – say, the intelligentsia, or 'literary circles'. No group has the right to its own opinion about some event or other. In matters of this kind there are fine points of etiquette which nobody can appreciate unless he has been in our shoes. Bukharin knew how to present things in the right way, and it was the postscript at the end of his letter that explained why Stalin chose to telephone Pasternak and not someone else. ...

Stalin began by telling Pasternak that Mandelstam's case had been reviewed, and that everything would be all right. This was followed by a strange reproach: why hadn't Pasternak approached the writers' organizations, or him (Stalin), and why hadn't he tried to do something for Mandelstam: 'If I were a poet and a poet friend of mine were in trouble, I would do anything to help him.'

Pasternak's reply to this was: 'The writers' organizations haven't bothered with cases like this since 1927, and if I hadn't tried to do something, you probably would never have heard about it.' Pasternak went on to say something about the word 'friend', trying to define more precisely the nature of his relations with M., which were not, of course, covered by the term 'friendship'. This digression was very much in Pasternak's style and had no relevance to the matter in hand. Stalin interrupted him: 'But he's a genius, he's a genius, isn't he?' To this Pasternak replied: 'But that's not the point.' 'What is it, then?' Stalin asked. Pasternak then said that he would like to meet him and have a talk. 'About what?' 'About life and death,' Pasternak replied. Stalin hung up. Pasternak tried to get him back, but could only reach a secretary. Stalin did not come to the phone again. Pasternak asked the secretary whether he could talk about this conversation or whether he should keep quiet about it. To his surprise, he was told he could talk about it as much as he liked – there was no need at all to make a secret of it. Stalin clearly wanted it to have the widest possible repercussions. A miracle is only a miracle, after all, if people stand in wonder before it.

Everybody could now clearly see what miracles Stalin was capable of, and it was to Pasternak that the honor had fallen not only of spreading the good tidings all over Moscow, but also of hearing a sermon in connection with it. The aim of the miracle was thus achieved: attention was diverted from the victim to the miracle-worker. It was extraordinarily symptomatic of the period that, in discussing the miracle, nobody thought to ask why Stalin should have rebuked Pasternak for not trying to save a friend and fellow poet while at the same time he was calmly sending his own friends and comrades to their death. Even Pasternak [who] had not thought about [his] contemporaries took Stalin's sermon on friendship between poets completely at its face value and was ecstatic about a ruler who had shown such warmth of spirit.

N. Mandelstam [37], pp. 145–7.

DOCUMENT 18   THE STALIN CULT BLOSSOMS

This extract is taken from a speech by A.O. Avdienko, a writer, to the VIIth Congress of Soviets in February 1935; the poem appeared in Pravda *in August 1936.*

Thank you, Stalin. Thank you because I am joyful. Thank you because I am well. No matter how old I become, I shall never forget how we received Stalin two days ago. Centuries will pass, and the generations still to come will regard us as the happiest of mortals, as the most fortunate of men, because we lived in the century of centuries, because we were privileged to see Stalin, our inspired leader. Yes, and we regard ourselves as the happiest of mortals because we are the contemporaries of a man who never had an equal in world history.

The men of all ages will call on thy name, which is strong, beautiful, wise and marvellous. Thy name is engraven on every factory, every machine, every place on the earth, and in the hearts of all men.

Every time I have found myself in his presence I have been subjugated by his strength, his charm, his grandeur. I have experienced a great desire to sing, to cry out, to shout with joy and happiness. And now see me – me! – on the same platform where the Great Stalin stood a year ago. In what country, in what part of the world could such a thing happen?

I write books. I am an author. All thanks to thee, O great educator, Stalin. I love a young woman with a renewed love and shall perpetuate myself in my children – all thanks to thee, great educator, Stalin. I shall be eternally happy and joyous, all thanks to thee, great educator, Stalin. Everything belongs to thee, chief of our great country. And when the woman I love presents me with a child the first word it shall utter will be: Stalin.

> O great Stalin, O leader of the peoples,
> Thou who broughtest man to birth.
> Thou who fructifiest the earth,
> Thou who restorest the centuries,
> Thou who makest bloom the spring,
> Thou who makest vibrate the musical chords ...
> Thou, splendour of my spring, O Thou,
> Sun reflected by millions of hearts ...

Pravda, 1 February 1935, 28 August 1936, Rigby [43], pp. 111–12.

DOCUMENT 19 (a) **A CALL TO ARMS**

The situation was desperate when Stalin delivered this radio speech on 3 July 1941. Right up to the moment of invasion the Soviet people had been assured that there would be no attack. Added to German destruction was the demand that if the Red Army had to retreat a scorched earth policy was to be adopted.

Comrades, citizens, brothers and sisters, men of our Army and Navy! It is to you I am speaking dear friends!

The perfidious military attack by Hitlerite Germany on our Motherland, begun on 22 June, is continuing. In spite of the heroic resistance of the Red Army, and although the enemy's finest divisions and finest air force units have already been smashed and have found their graves on the field of battle, the enemy continues to push forward, hurling fresh forces to the front. Hitler's troops have succeeded in capturing Lithuania, a considerable part of Latvia, the western part of Byelorussia and part of Western Ukraine. The Fascist aircraft are extending the range of their operations. ... Grave danger overhangs our country.

The Red Army, Red Navy and all citizens of the Soviet Union must defend every inch of Soviet soil, must fight to the last drop of blood for our towns and villages, must display the daring, initiative and mental alertness characteristic of our people. ...

We must strengthen the Red Army's rear, subordinating all our work to this end; all our industries must be got to work with greater intensity, to produce more rifles, machine-guns, cartridges, shells, planes; we must organize the guarding of factories, power stations, telephonic and telegraphic communications, and arrange local air-raid protection.

We must wage a ruthless fight against all disorganizers of the rear, deserters, panic-mongers and rumor-mongers; we must exterminate spies, sabotage agents and enemy parachutists, rendering rapid aid in all this to our extermination battalions. We must bear in mind that the enemy is treacherous, cunning, experienced in deception and the dissemination of false rumours. We must reckon with all this, and not fall victims to provocation. All who by their panic-mongering and cowardice hinder the work of defence, no matter who they may be, must be immediately hauled before a military tribunal.

In case of a forced retreat of Red Army units, all rolling-stock must be evacuated, the enemy must not be left a single engine, a single railway truck, not a single pound of grain or gallon of fuel. Collective farmers must drive off all their cattle and turn over their grain to the safe keeping of the State authorities, for transportation to the rear. All valuable property, including non-ferrous metals, grain and fuel that cannot be withdrawn, must be destroyed without fail.

In areas occupied by the enemy, partisan units, mounted and foot, must be formed; sabotage groups must be organized to combat enemy units, to foment partisan warfare everywhere, blow up bridges and roads, damage telephone and telegraph lines, set fire to forests, stores and transports. In occupied regions conditions must be made unbearable for the enemy and all his accomplices. They must be hounded and annihilated at every step, and all their measures frustrated.

Soviet Foreign Policy during the Patriotic War [159].

(b) REAL BURDEN OF DEFENCE OUTLAYS,
1940–44 (billion roubles at 1937 factor cost)

The Soviet Union paid a heavier price in human and material resources during the war than any other belligerent country.

	1940	1941	1942	1943	1944
GDP	247.6	206.3	144.1	160.9	192.2
Net imports	0.0	0.0	9.0	30.9	35.6
Defence outlays:	45.3	66.9	110.1	133.8	145.3
Munitions	16.6	28.3	61.6	82.3	90.2
Pay	6.8	9.8	15.8	16.6	17.2
Food	9.9	14.1	16.1	19.0	19.1
Clothing, etc.	4.4	5.1	6.4	5.3	6.3
Fuel	1.5	2.1	2.4	2.7	3.1
Transport	0.9	1.1	1.4	2.6	3.0
Construction	2.4	2.6	2.0	1.1	1.5
Other, including repairs	2.7	3.8	4.5	4.2	4.8
Defence outlays, less net imports	45.3	66.9	101.1	102.9	109.7
Defence outlays, % of GDP:					
Domestic supply	18.0	32.0	70.0	64.0	57.0
Foreign supply	0.0	0.0	6.0	19.0	19.0

M. Harrison [81], Table 4 and D-1.

(c) MILITARY LOSSES IN THE GREAT PATRIOTIC WAR (millions)

1.	Killed in action and died of injuries before reaching a hospital	5.227
2.	Died from injuries in hospitals	1.103
3.	Died from disease, accident or shot as punishment (of whom	0.556

	died from diseases	0.267
	died from accidents and shootings	0.289)
4.	Missing and imprisoned (according to military reports	
	and the data of the repatriation organs)	3.396
5.	Unaccounted for losses in the first months of war	1.163
6.	Total losses (1 + 2 + 3 + 4 + 5)	11.444

Less

7.	Previously surrounded and missing soldiers subsequently called	
	up on liberated territory	0.940
8.	Returned prisoners of war	1.836
9.	Total (7 + 8)	2.776
10.	Net loss (6 - 9)	8.668
	of whom	
	not returned from imprisonment (died,	
	killed, emigrated)	1.783
	armed forces	8.509
	frontier troops	0.061
	internal troops	0.098

M. Ellman and S. Maksudov [73], p. 674.

DOCUMENT 20 (a) **GDP PER HEAD OF THE USSR IN INTERNATIONAL COMPARISON,** 1913–40 ($ and 1980 prices)

The Soviet Union was ahead of Japan in GDP per head in 1913 but behind in 1940. Apart from Japan, however, the USSR was growing faster than the other economies. This was partly due to the fact that mature economies grow more slowly than those which begin from a low base. Real GDP by sector of origin reveals that industry by 1944 contributed almost as much as in 1937 – a formidable achievement given the war and dislocation.

	1913	1928	1932	1937	1940
Japan	800	1150	1130	1330	1660
Russia (USSR)	900	900	930	1440	1440
Italy	1550	1780	1740	1960	2070
Germany	1960	2280	1880	2740	3190
France	2000	2550	2280	2590	2330
UK	2970	3110	2990	3610	3980
USA	3790	4690	3450	4570	4970

R.W. Davies et al. [70], p. 270.

(b) REAL GDP BY SECTOR OF ORIGIN,
1937–44 (billion roubles and 1937 factor cost)

	1937	1940	1941	1942	1943	1944
Agriculture	63.0	69.9	42.3	25.3	30.4	45.0
Industry:	65.4	73.8	70.3	51.1	59.2	66.5
defence industry	3.4	8.3	14.2	28.1	35.0	38.7
civilian industry	62.0	65.5	56.2	22.9	24.2	27.8
Construction	10.5	10.6	6.9	3.2	3.4	4.4
Transport, communications	16.8	19.3	17.8	10.2	11.8	13.7
Trade, catering	10.4	11.1	9.3	3.8	3.5	4.1
Civilian services	33.1	42.0	35.3	22.1	23.4	28.8
Military services:	3.7	7.3	10.4	16.6	17.3	17.9
army, navy	3.4	6.8	9.8	15.8	16.6	17.2
NKVD	0.3	0.5	0.6	0.8	0.7	0.7
NDP	202.9	234.0	192.3	132.4	149.1	180.5
Depreciation	9.4	13.6	14.0	11.7	11.8	11.7
GDP	212.3	247.6	206.3	144.1	160.9	192.2

M. Harrison [81], Table 1.

DOCUMENT 21   (a) *PRIKAZ* (DECREE) OF THE USSR
PEOPLE'S COMMISSARIAT OF INTERNAL
AFFAIRS ISSUED IN 1941

This is the decree (prikaz*) deporting ethnic Germans from the Volga
German Republic, Saratov and Stalingrad oblasts mainly to Siberia and
Kazakhstan. They were accused of conspiring with the advancing
Wehrmacht troops. Ethnic Germans in the Red Army, the party and other
institutions were also affected. The Germans were absolved of all blame by
Khrushchev but their republic was never returned to them. They, together
with the Crimean Tatars, are the only two deported nationalities which did
not receive their old territory back. In all, about 52 nationalities were
deported in the 1940s. Recent Russian estimates put the number exiled or
resettled between 1941 and 1948 at about 3.3 million with another 215,000
being despatched later. Besides storing up hatred of Russians and the Soviet
regime, these deportations had an unexpected consequence. They forced
disparate nationalities from the North Caucasus and Transcaucasia to
cooperate to survive. Some of the mafia gangs of the 1980s and 1990s in
Russian began in embryo in exile.*

001158. Contents: Measures on the Deportation of Germans from the Volga German Republic and Saratov and Stalingrad Oblasts
No.001158 August 27, 1941 Moscow

In order to execute the Decree of USSR Sovnarkom and CC RCP(B) on the deportation of Germans from the Volga German Republic, Saratov and Stalingrad oblasts, the following measures are to be carried out:

1. Send a USSR NKVD operational group headed by Comrade Serov, USSR Deputy People's Commissar of Internal Affairs, to the area. ...

2. Entrust the following troikas [group of three] with the task of preparing and carrying out the operation in the oblasts. ...

3. On arrival at the designated place, the three responsible officials are to organise the operation. Carry out the operation according to the appended instructions.

4. The operation is to begin on September 3 and is to be completed on September 20, 1941.

5. Send special USSR NKVD officers to each settlement area for German deportees and make them responsible for preparing the timely acceptance of columns with the deportees at the transfer points and in the settlement areas. ...

6. To carry out the deportation operation, Comrade Obruchnikov, Deputy People's Commissar, is to send 1200 NKVD officers and 2000 militia officials to the Volga German Republic; 250 special NKVD officials and 1000 militia officials to Saratov Oblast; 100 NKVD officers and 250 militia officials to Stalingrad Oblast.

7. To carry out the deportation operation by the NKVD troops, Major-General Apollonov is to send Brigade Commissar Krivenko and 7350 Red Army soldiers, under his command, to the Volga German Republic; Colonel Vorobeikov and 2300 Red Army soldiers, under his command, to Saratov Oblast; Brigade Commissar Sladkevich and 2500 Red Army soldiers, under his command, to Stalingrad Oblast.
   Deputy People's Commissar Obruchnikov and Major-General Apollonov are to ensure that those sent officially arrive at the place designated for them not later than September 1, 1941.

8. To ensure the embarquement of German deportees on steamers in Astrakhan, Comrade Voronin, Head of the Stalingrad NKVD Administration is to provide an operational group to help the Astrakhan Section for Operatives.

9. On the basis of the information received by local NKVD organs from agents and operatives, identify anti-Soviet elements and arrest them before the operation and deport their families in the conventional manner.

10.   Prior to the operation, explain the situation to Soviet and Party activists and warn the deportees that if they assume an illegal status, some members will be prosecuted and other family members will be subjected to repression [execution or imprisonment].

11.   If some family members to be deported refuse to go to the settlement area, arrest such persons and transfer them forcibly to the settlement area.

12.   Warn all NKVD personnel involved in the operation that the operation is not to be accompanied by noise or panic. If any delays, anti-Soviet actions or armed clashes occur, take decisive measures to eliminate them.

13.   To coordinate the whole deportation, transfer and settling procedure, Comrade Chernyshov, USSR Deputy People's Commissar of Internal Affairs, Comrade Fedotov, head of the Red Army Administration and Comrade Sinegubov, Head of the Transport Administration are to be seconded to the USSR NKVD.

14.   Comrade Serov, Deputy People's Commissar, is to inform the USSR NKVD* on the preparation and the progress of the operation beginning from September 1, 1941.

L. Beria, USSR People's
Commissar of Internal Affairs,
General Commissar of State
Security

[*According to the data of the USSR NKVD Section of Special Deportation Areas, 446,480 persons were deported from the regions mentioned in the *prikaz*, In addition to the Germans from the Volga German Republic, more than 800,000 citizens of German nationality who were living scattered throughout the country had been deported.]

TsGAOR, f. 8331, op. 22, d. 542, l. 234.

(b) THE USSR NKVD SECTION FOR COMBATING BANDITRY

An Extract from an Explanatory Note by Lavrenty Beria to Comrade J.V. Stalin, Comrade V.M. Molotov (USSR Sovnarkom) and Comrade G.M. Malenkov (CC, RCP (b)).

July 1944

In order to implement the decree of the State Committee of Defence, 602,193 inhabitants of the North Caucasus, of whom 496,460 were Chechens and Ingushi, 68,327 were Karachai and 37,406 were Balkars, were deported by the NKVD for permanent residence in Kazakhstan and Kirgizia, in February–March 1944.

Most of the special deportees (477,809 persons) were sent to Kazakhstan. However, the republican agencies of Kazakhstan did not devote due attention to the problem of providing special deportees from the North Caucasus with gardens and household plots. As a result, the living standards of special deportees in Kazakhstan and their engagement in socially useful labour have been unsatisfactory. Special deportees' families settled in kolkhozes were not allowed to join agricultural artels [cooperatives]. The provision of special deportees with household plots and gardens and also living quarters was inadequate. Special deportees settled in sovkhozes and assigned to industrial enterprises were unsatisfactorily employed in industrial enterprises. Cases of typhus, shortcomings in the provision of household plots and in living conditions, thefts and criminal offences were recorded.

In order to introduce proper order, Kruglov, USSR Deputy People's Commissar of Internal Affairs, and a group of officers were sent on an official visit in May 1944 to Kazakhstan. In July 1944 2,196 special deportees were arrested for various offences. All the cases were heard by special courts. 429 NKVD special komendaturas were established to supervise the residence conditions of the special deportees, combat escapes, provide NKVD operatives and provide as quickly as possible special deportees' families with household plots.

Special deportees were provided with better and larger household plots. Of 70,296 families settled in kolkhozes, 56,800 or 81 per cent became members of agricultural artels; 83,303 families (74.3 per cent) received household plots and gardens; 12,683 families lived in their own houses. The work of children's labour colonies was organised. In June 1944 1,268 children were placed there. More special deportees were employed. For example, of a total of 16,927 persons found capable of work, 16,396 were actually employed in Dzhambul oblast. In Akmolinsk oblast of 19,345 persons, 17,667 were actually working and of these 2,746 were old people and children.

TsGAOR, f. 9479, op. 1, d. 228, l. 259–67.

DOCUMENT 22   **THE COST OF HOSTILITIES: A BALANCE SHEET**

The euphoria [of victory] however, concealed an appalling bill of costs. Outstanding among these were the 27 million to 28 million premature deaths incurred by the Soviet population, which accounted for no fewer than one in seven of the prewar population, and up to half of global demographic losses attributable to World War II.

The bleeding wounds of victory were everywhere. The Soviet Army had lost nearly 9 million dead. No other army in history had achieved so much at such great cost. The civilian cost was still greater. Some 19 million civilians had perished before their time. One-third of the prewar capital stock had been destroyed, and twice that amount used up by wartime defence, economic conversion, and lost national income. ...

In the years just after the war, the reinforced legitimacy of Stalin and Stalinist institutions ran strongly against other, weaker currents welling up from below. The war experience would also supply a smothered impulse to reform. There was a widespread desire for liberalisation and relaxation, in politics as in culture and economic affairs. Veterans of military service and war work, whose loyalty to the Soviet system had passed the severest test, may have expected the system to reward them with greater trust and increased rights of participation, not just free bus passes. Some also believed that the war had revealed the weaknesses of Stalinist dictatorship, above all in 1941–2, and the necessity of limiting the arbitrary powers of individual leaders. The war had given many the opportunity to exercise their own personal initiative and responsibility on a wider scale than in peacetime, as military commanders, factory managers, farmers, war administrators, war writers and reporters, and had taught them that mere unthinking obedience to superior orders was not enough.

For the time being, however, such beliefs and values would remain implicit or, if voiced *en clair*, dangerous to the individuals who held them. Among the political leadership there were only confused ideological shadings, without sharp distinctions between overall political alternatives or coherent programmes. In the absence of any clear challenge, Stalin would seek to restore everything as it was before the war to the rigid mould of personal dictatorship and rule from above by decree. And while he lived he would very largely succeed. Other nations – the two Germanies and Japan under Allied occupation, Britain under the Attlee government, France and Italy under new postwar constitutions – went through different postwar reforms. In the Soviet Union, in contrast, the prewar order of forced industrial accumulation, political dictatorship, and social mobilisation, would be restored. ...

If not Stalin, then who can be credited with the great victory on the eastern front? Millions of ordinary people, infantrymen, officers, workers at the bench and in the field, managers, writers – even war administrators and Party secretaries: these shouldered the main burdens, whether they did it well or badly. For the most part they were not born great heroes, and they were not innately brave or noble, although many of them did very brave things. They were marked out not by special personal qualities but by special circumstances, and an extraordinary history.

What enabled them to wage such a terrible war and emerge victorious? The answer to these questions is the same – everything in their history, their revolutionary and national traditions, their cultural ties and family roles, the social, economic and administrative webs which defined their place in Soviet life, the organs of state, the Party and its leaders, and Stalin too. All these are indispensable elements of the explanation of what made them fight, and why victory cost them so much.

J.D. Barber and M. Harrison [62], pp. 206–11.

DOCUMENT 23   STALIN THE OMNISCIENT

Stalin is the brilliant leader and teacher of the Party, the great strategist of the Socialist Revolution, military commander, the guide of the Soviet state. An implacable attitude towards the enemies of Socialism, profound fidelity to principle, a combination of clear revolutionary perspective and clarity of purpose with extraordinary firmness and persistence in the pursuit of aims, wise and practical leadership, and intimate contact with the masses – such are the characteristic features of Stalin's style. After Lenin, no other leader in the world had been called upon to direct such vast masses of workers and peasants. He has a unique faculty for generalizing the constructive revolutionary experience of the masses, for seizing upon and developing their initiative, for learning from the masses as well as teaching them, and for leading them forward to victory.

Stalin's whole career is an example of profound theoretical power combined with an unusual breadth and versatility of practical experience in the revolutionary struggle.

In conjunction with the tried and tested Leninists who are his immediate associates, and at the head of the great Bolshevik Party, Stalin guides the destinies of a multi-national Socialist state, a state of workers and peasants of which there is no precedent in history. His advice is taken as a guide to action in all fields of Socialist construction. His work is extraordinary for its variety; his energy truly amazing. The range of questions which engage his attention is immense, embracing complex problems of Marxist–Leninist theory and school textbooks; problems of Soviet foreign policy and the municipal affairs of Moscow, the proletarian capital; the development of the Great Northern Sea Route and the reclamation of the Colchian marshes; the advancement of Soviet literature and art and the editing of the model rules for collective farms; and, lastly, the solution of most intricate theoretical and practical problems in the science of warfare.

Everybody is familiar with the cogent and invincible force of Stalin's logic, the crystal clarity of his mind, his iron will, his devotion to the party, his ardent faith in the people, and love for the people. Everybody is familiar with his modesty, his simplicity of manner, his consideration for people, and his merciless severity towards enemies of the people. Everybody is familiar with his intolerance of ostentation, of phrasemongers and windbags, of whiners and alarmists. Stalin is wise and deliberate in solving complex political questions where a thorough weighing of pros and cons is required.

At the same time, he is a supreme master of bold revolutionary decisions and of swift adaptations to changed conditions.

Stalin is the worthy continuer of the cause of Lenin, or, as it is said in the Party: Stalin is the Lenin of today.

G.F. Alexandrov, et al. [15], pp. 198–201.

DOCUMENT 24   STALIN ON RED ARMY DISCIPLINE

Do you see what a complicated thing is man's soul, his psyche? Well then, imagine a man who has fought from Stalingrad to Belgrade – over thousands of kilometres of his own devastated land, across the dead bodies of his comrades and dearest ones! How can such a man react normally? And what is so awful in his amusing himself with a woman, after such horrors? You have imagined the Red Army to be ideal. And it is not ideal, or can it be, even if it did not contain a certain percentage of criminals – we opened up our prisons and stuck everybody into the army. There was an interesting case. An Air Force major wanted to have a woman, and a chivalrous engineer appeared to protect her. The major drew a gun: 'Ech, you mole from the rear!' – and he killed the chivalrous engineer. They sentenced the major to death. But somehow the matter was brought before me, and I made inquiries – I have the right as commander in chief in time of war – and I released the major and sent him to the front. Now he is one of our heroes. One has to understand the soldier. The Red Army is not ideal. The important thing is that it fights Germans – and it is fighting them well; the rest doesn't matter.

Soon afterwards when I returned from Moscow, I heard, to my horror, of a far more significant example of Stalin's 'understanding' attitude toward the sins of Red Army personnel. While crossing East Prussia, Soviet soldiers, especially the tank units, had regularly shelled and killed all the German civilian refugees – women and children. Stalin was informed of this and asked what should be done. He replied: 'We lecture our soldiers too much; let them have some initiative!'

M. Djilas [24], pp. 101–2.

DOCUMENT 25   STALIN IN 1948

I could hardly believe how much he had changed in two or three years. When I had last seen him, in 1945, he was still lively, quick-witted, and had a pointed sense of humour. But that was during the war and it had been it would seem, Stalin's last effort and had taken him to his limit. Now he laughed at inanities and shallow jokes. On one occasion he not only failed to get the political point of an anecdote I told him about how he had got the better of Churchill and Roosevelt, but he even seemed to be offended, as old men sometimes are. I perceived an embarrassed astonishment on the faces of the rest of the party.

In one thing, though, he was still the Stalin of old: stubborn, sharp, suspicious whenever anyone disagreed with him. He even cut Molotov, and one could feel the tension between them. Everyone paid court to him, avoiding any expression of opinion before he expressed his, and then hastening to agree with him. ...

Toward the end of the dinner Stalin unexpectedly asked me why there were not many Jews in the Yugoslav Party and why these few played no important role in it. I tried to explain to him that there were not many Jews in Yugoslavia to begin with, and most belonged to the middle class. I added, 'The only prominent Communist Jew is Pijade, and he regards himself as being more of a Serb than a Jew'.

Stalin began to recall: 'Pijade, short, with glasses? Yes, I remember, he visited me. And what is his position?'

'He is a member of the Central Committee, a veteran Communist, the translator of *Das Kapital*', I explained.

'In our Central Committee there are no Jews!' he broke in, and began to laugh tauntingly. 'You are an anti-Semite, you, too, Djilas, you, too, are an anti-Semite!'

I took his words and laughter to mean the opposite, as I should have – as the expression of his own anti-Semitism and as a provocation to get me to declare my stand concerning the Jews, particularly Jews in the Communist movement.

M. Djilas [24], pp. 138–40.

DOCUMENT 26   SOVIET ATTITUDES TOWARDS YUGOSLAV
CULTURE

How little the views of the Yugoslavs were respected can be seen from an incident which happened to Tito while he was in Moscow. He says:

'The representatives of the Soviet press asked me to write an article for their papers. I did so, and when I got the text, I noticed that eight-tenths of my views had been completely altered according to the wishes of the editors. I was already familiar with such methods in the Soviet Union, but I never imagined that Soviet journalists could alter to their own formula the text of an article written by the Prime Minister of a friendly allied country. The same thing happened to Djilas, Moša Pijade, and Rato Dugonjić, the Secretary of the People's Youth of Yugoslavia. The latter had written an article about the Brčko–Banovići railway which the youth of Yugoslavia had built by voluntary work. The editor of *Komsomolskaya Pravda* changed the article considerably, even shortening the railway from fifty miles to thirty-seven. Strange logic!'

In contacts with the most responsible Soviet representatives a tone of disparagement towards the Yugoslavs as a people was noticeable, disparagement of our culture, complete ignorance of our history and our way of life. For instance, Zhdanov once asked Djilas whether opera existed in Yugoslavia. There were twelve opera houses in Yugoslavia, and Yugoslav composers, Lisinski for instance, had been writing operas more than a century ago. It was not merely a matter of belittling our culture, our language, and our press in words, but also in deeds. The Soviet representatives in Yugoslavia proposed that we should include as many Russian songs in our radio programmes as possible. Had we accepted their suggestion there would have been two or three times as many Russian songs as Yugoslav. They also asked us to increase the number of Russian plays in our theatres. We have always esteemed Gogol, Ostrovsky, Gorki, but we refused to flood our theatres with third-rate modern Soviet plays. As for films, in 1946 they imposed on us a block booking contract, so that we had no choice of the films they sent; and we had to pay the rental in dollars, at three, four, or five times the prices we paid for films from the West. Thus we got Laurence Olivier's *Hamlet* for about two thousand dollars but for *Exploits of a Soviet Intelligence Agent* we had to pay some twenty thousand dollars.

Various Soviet representatives especially pounced on our press as one of the most powerful instruments of propaganda. Almost every week a representative of the Soviet Information Bureau would come round with several hundred articles written in Moscow on various topics, mostly about life in the Soviet Union, birthdays of Russian writers, composers, and scientists, or life in the collectives; there were also many articles about other countries, and he persistently asked for all this material to be published in our dailies and weeklies. Had we printed them all, we should have had almost no space left for our own journalists, who would soon have been out of work, leaving the people to be informed of world events only through the eyes of writers in Moscow.

On the other hand, we asked the Soviet government to publish at least something about Yugoslavia in the Soviet press, on a reciprocal basis. This was always avoided. Some articles waited a year for publication, then were returned without having seen daylight. The same thing happened with books. We published 1,850 Soviet books; they published two of ours.

V. Dedijer [22], pp. 274–5.

DOCUMENT 27 THE IMPORTANCE OF THE COW

This was why I dreamed of a cow. Thanks to the vagaries of our economic system, a family could support itself for many years by keeping a cow. Millions lived in wretched huts, feeding themselves from the products of their tiny plots of land (on which they grew potatoes, cabbage, cucumbers, beets, turnips and onions) and their cow. Some of the milk had to be sold to buy hay, but there was always enough left over to add a little richness to the cabbage soup. A cow gives people some independence and, without over-exerting themselves, they can earn a little extra to buy bread. The State is still in a quandary about this relic of the old world: if people are allowed to buy hay to feed their cow, then they do only the very minimum of work on the kolkhoz; if, on the other hand, you take their cows away, they will die of hunger. The result is that the cow is alternately forbidden and then permitted again.

N. Mandelstam [37], p. 301.

DOCUMENT 28 A JEWISH SUCCESS STORY

It was Lezhnev who had asked M. to write *The Noise of Time* for *Rossia*, but then turned it down after reading it – he had expected a totally different kind of childhood story, such as he himself was later to write. His was the story of a Jewish boy from the shtetl who discovers Marxism. He was lucky with his book. At first nobody wanted to publish it – though it was probably no worse than others of its kind – but then it was read and approved by Stalin. Stalin even tried to phone Lezhnev to tell him, but Lezhnev was not at home at the moment Stalin called. When he learned what had happened, Lezhnev sat by his phone for a whole week, hoping that Stalin might ring back. But miracles, as we know, are not repeated. A week later he was informed that there would be no further telephone call, but that orders had been given for his book to be published (it was already being printed), that he had been made a member of the Party on Stalin's personal recommendation and appointed editor of *Pravda's* literary section. In this way Lezhnev, hitherto a nobody who could always be trampled underfoot as a former private publisher, was suddenly raised to the greatest heights and almost went crazy from joy and emotion. Of all the Haroun al Rashid miracles, this, incidentally, turned out to be the most enduring: Lezhnev kept his *Pravda* post, or an equivalent one, right up to his death.

On hearing all this, Lezhnev at last left his telephone and rushed off to the barber – his beard had grown considerably during the week of waiting. Next he called on us to present us with *The Dialectic of Nature* and to tell us about the great change that Marxism had brought into his life. None of this had ever entered his head in the days when he was editor of *Rossia*. From what he said, it appeared that he had read some newly discovered works by Engels, notably *The Dialectic of Nature,* and seen the light. He had even gone into a bookshop just now and bought a copy for us, because he hoped it would help M. to see the light as well. Lezhnev was an exceptionally sincere and well-meaning person. I was even a little envious of him at that moment – a genuine conversion to the true faith, which suddenly puts an end to all your troubles and at the same time starts bringing in a regular income, must be a remarkably agreeable thing.

N. Mandelstam [37], pp. 241–2.

DOCUMENT 29 **THE REALITY OF SOVIET PLANNING**

Zaleski here argues that the central national plan, from which all other plans are derived, was a myth.

In describing the Soviet economy – a centrally planned economy – the tendency is to give planning priority over management. This would be correct if the central plan, broken down among economic units in an authoritarian fashion, were actually carried out. However, this study shows that the existence of such a central national plan, coherent and perfect, to be subdivided and implemented at all levels, is only a *myth*. What actually exists, as in any centrally administered economy, is an endless number of plans, constantly evolving, that are coordinated *ex post* after they have been put into operation. The unification of these innumerable plans into a single national plan, supposedly coherent, takes place rarely (once or twice during a five-year period and once for an annual or quarterly plan); furthermore, the attempt at unification is only a projection of observed tendencies resulting from extrapolating trends based on natural forces.

In view of the changing and often ephemeral nature of the plans, management emerges as the only constant in the system. The economic administration is built on a strict hierarchy descending from the ministry (or people's commissariat) to the enterprise, subject to strict discipline, obeying orders transmitted continuously. Under each management agency, from the Council of Ministers down to the enterprises, there is a planning commission with a consulting role. ... Of course, higher-level 'consultants' (Gosplan) tend to take over certain management functions (material and equipment supply) or to intervene more or less directly in management, but then they become administrators just like the others and their 'planning' becomes management.

The priority of management over planning has been the dominant feature of the Soviet economy since Stalin's time. Since management is highly centralized, this feature is characteristic of the entire model. Therefore, it seems more nearly correct to call the economy 'centrally managed' rather than centrally planned.

E. Zaleski [105], p. 484.

DOCUMENT 30 STALINISM LIVES ON

There were still Soviet citizens who looked back to the Stalin era with nostalgia. In those days this worker enjoyed self-respect and had a purpose in life – which he later lost.

I remember one of my neighbours in Pskov, a house painter and former partisan who is still a die-hard Stalinist. Every day he came home swearing obscenely and shouting in the corridor of our communal apartment about how good things had been under Stalin. Then his wife would drag him off to the room where they lived with their two children, but we could still hear his drunken praise of Stalin: 'He gave me an apartment, he gave me a medal, he gave me my self-respect. ... You know who I mean. ... He lowered the prices. ...'

N. Mandelstam [37], p. 254.

DOCUMENT 31 WHAT IS STALINISM?

There are many different approaches to a study of the Stalinist system. There is the totalitarian or intentionalist approach which concentrates on politics and ideology, the strong state and strong leader; the Stalinist Marxist approach which views Stalinism as the dictatorship of the proletariat; the Trotskyist approach which emphasises the trend to Thermidorian bureaucracy and the emergence of a Leviathan state; the state capitalist approach which sees a nominally socialist state but run along capitalist lines (workers as wage labour); the new class approach of Djilas; the oriental despotism interpretation of Karl Wittfogel, who argues that traditions of deference to authority may have had their origins in the high levels of socio-political organisation required by a 'hydraulic society' in which the office of watermaster (controller of irrigation water) in arid lands was sovereign; the pluralist approach, which includes institutional pluralism; the corporatist interpretation; and finally the industrial society approach which concentrates on the primacy of industrialisation.

(a)

1. Commitment to a violent anti-capitalist revolution which *does not develop beyond* the replacement of the political power of the bourgeoisie by the power of *political bureacracy* and of private property by *state ownership* of the means of production.

2. The leading force of the revolution and the backbone of the post-revolutionary society is a *monolithic, strongly disciplined, strictly hierarchical party* which has a *monopoly* of all economic and political power and *reduces all other* social organisations to its *mere transmissions.*

3. The state tends to exist even after the complete liquidation of a capitalist class. Its primary new function is a *rigid administrative* planning of all production and complete control of all political life. The state is officially a dictatorship of the working class; in reality it is *dictatorship of the party leadership or of one single leader*.

4. The new society is continued as a *collectivist welfare* society in which most forms of *economic and political alienation* would survive.

5. As a consequence of the centralist political and economic structure, smaller nations in a multi-national country are *denied self-determination* and continue to be *dominated* by the biggest nation.

6. *All culture is subordinated to the sphere of politics* and is strictly controlled and censored by the ruling party.

Mihailo Marković, 'Stalinism and Marxism' in Tucker, ed. [51], p. 300.

(b)

Stalinism was not simply nationalism, bureaucratisation, absence of democracy, censorship, police repression and the rest in any precedented sense. These phenomena have appeared in many societies and are rather easily explained.

Instead Stalinism was excess, extraordinary extremism, in each. It was not, for example, merely coercive peasant policies, but a virtual civil war against the peasantry; not merely police repression, or even civil war style terror, but a holocaust by terror that victimised tens of millions of people for twenty five years; not merely a Thermidorian revival of nationalist tradition, but an almost fascist-like chauvinism; not merely a leader cult, but deification of a despot. ... Excesses were the essence of historical Stalinism, and they are what really require explanation.

Stephen F. Cohen, 'Bolshevism and Stalinism' in Tucker, ed. [51], pp. 12–13.

(c)

The cult of the state and worship of rank, the irresponsibility of those who hold power and the population's lack of rights, the hierarchy of privileges and the canonisation of hypocrisy, the barrack system of social and intellectual life, the suppression of the individual and the destruction of independent thought, the environment of terror and suspicion, the atomisation of people and the notorious 'vigilance', the uncontrolled violence and the legalised cruelty.

R.A. Medvedev [7], p. 553.

(d)

(i) A formally highly centralised, directive economic system characterised by mass mobilisation and an overriding priority on the development of heavy industry;

(ii) A social structure initially characterised by significant fluidity, most particularly in the form of high levels of social mobility which brings the former lower classes into positions of power and privilege; subsequent consolidation of the social structure results in the dominance of rank, status and hierarchy;

(iii) A cultural and intellectual sphere in which all elements are meant to serve the political aims laid down by the leadership and where all areas of culture and intellectual production are politically monitored;

(iv) A personal dictatorship resting upon the use of terror as an instrument of rule and in which the political institutions are little more than the instrument of the dictator;

(v) All spheres of life are politicised, hence, within the scope of state concerns;

(vi) The centralisation of authority is paralleled by a significant measure of weakness of continuing central control, resulting in a system which, in practice, is in its daily operations loosely controlled and structured;

(vii) The initial revolutionary ethos is superseded by a profoundly conservative, status quo, orientation.

G. Gill [27], pp. 57–8.

GLOSSARY

ASSR Autonomous Soviet Socialist Republic; an administrative unit of a republic which is populated by a nationality other than the titular nationality: e.g. the Tatars made up the Tatar ASSR in the RSFSR. Although they had their own government, they were ruled from the titular nationality's capital; in the Tatars case, Moscow. Hence 'autonomous' here does not mean independent.

AUSW All-Russian Union of Soviet Writers; *see also* AUW and RAPP.

AUW All-Russian Union of Writers; *see also* AUSW and RAPP.

Bolsheviks When the All-Russian Social Democratic Labour Party (RSDRP), founded in 1898, split in 1903, those in the majority became known as Bolsheviks; in October 1917 the Bolshevik or communist party seized power.

Brest-Litovsk Brest-Litovsk Treaty with Germany, March 1918, recognised Soviet Russia in international law; fulfilled the Bolshevik pledge to bring peace; revealed how split the Bolshevik leadership could be on a major issue.

candidate member (a) Before a person could become a full member of the Communist Party he had to serve a probationary period during which he was called a candidate member; (b) candidate members of the Central Committee and Politburo might attend meetings, speak but not vote.

CC Central Committee of the Communist Party; this organisation acted in the name of the Party Congress when the latter was not in session; it contained all the important party officials, government ministers, leading army and naval personnel, key ambassadors, etc.

CEC All-Russian Central Executive Committee of the soviets; the body which acted in the name of the Congress of Soviets when that body was not in session; theoretically, it was the supreme organ in the state but it rapidly lost power to *Sovnarkom* after December 1917. The Bolsheviks had a majority in the CEC but in the Presidium or inner council of the CEC there were only Bolsheviks; the chairman of the CEC was, in practice, the president of the country; in 1922 it changed its name to the CEC of the USSR; the 1936 constitution replaced it with the USSR Supreme Soviet. It was headed by L.B. Kamenev, October 1917–January 1918; Ya.M. Sverdlov, January 1918–March 1919; M.I. Kalinin, March 1919–36.

Cheka All-Russian Extraordinary Commission to Fight Counter Revolution, Sabotage and Speculation; established December 1917; renamed OGPU in 1922; later KGB.

collectivisation Establishment of *kolkhozes* and *sovkhozes*, which meant the end of private farming. Collectivisation began in 1917 but had made little impact by 1929 when it really got under way; was completed by 1937. In practice several villages were lumped together and declared a *kolkhoz*; peasant opposition was dealt with brutally, by using military force, deportation or expulsion; initially almost everything was collectivised, but in March 1930 the private plot around the peasant's cottage was legalised; as of May 1932 he could legally sell any surplus (after paying taxes) in an urban *kolkhoz* market where demand and supply determined prices.

Cominform Communist Information Bureau; established in 1947 and disbanded in 1955.

Comintern Communist International; international communist organisation established in 1919 and disbanded in 1943.

commissar (a) government minister; (b) official representing party, government or soviet.

Conference Differed from a Party Congress in that not all organisations were represented (an exception was the XIX Party Conference in 1988). In the early years the problems of logistics were such as to make it difficult to call a Congress at short notice. A Conference did not have the right to elect members to the Central Committee and Politburo.

Congress Most important meeting of party, soviet, trade union or other organisation; at a congress the Communist Party reviewed its past record and laid down goals for the future; a new Central Committee was elected and it, in turn, elected a new Politburo and Secretariat.

FYP Five-Year Plan; first FYP ran from October 1928 to December 1932; second from January 1933 to December 1937; third from January 1938 to June 1941; fourth from January 1946 to December 1950; fifth from January 1951 to December 1955.

GKO State Committee of Defence during the Great Fatherland War (1941–45).

Gosplan State Planning Commission of the USSR Council of Ministers; responsible for drafting economic plans and checking on their implementation; founded February 1921; headed by G.M. Krzhizhanovsky, 1921–23, 1925–30; A.D. Tsyurupa, 1923–25; V.V. Kuibyshev, 1930–34; V.I. Mezhlauk, 1934–37; N.A. Voznesensky, 1938–49.

kolkhoz Collective farm; members farmed the land as a cooperative but in reality had little say in what was to be produced; this was laid down in the annual state plan. Under Stalin payment was based on the number of labour days worked (it was possible to acquire several labour days during a day's work) and rewards came at the end of the harvest. If the farm recorded a loss no wages were paid. A basic guaranteed wage was only introduced in 1966.

kolkhoznik Collective farm peasant; between 1929 and 1966 there was no guaranteed basic wage; wages were paid out at end of harvest according to the profitability of the farm; the private plot kept the *kolkhoznik* and his family alive until the 1950s.

kombedy Committees of poor peasants; established by the Soviet government in June 1918 to seize grain from richer peasants who held surpluses; state was to get most of grain (to feed cities) but in fact received little. In November 1918 there were 122,000 *kombedy* but in the same month all were disbanded.

Komsomol Communist youth movement for those between ages fourteen and twenty-eight.

KPD Communist Party of Germany; founded in December 1919; refounded in Soviet Zone of Germany June 1945; fused with Soviet Zone SPD in April 1946 to form Socialist Unity Party of Germany (SED).

kulak peasants were divided into poor, middle and rich by the Bolsheviks; the poor peasant did not have enough land to live off, the middle peasant did, and the rich peasant had enough to produce a surplus; in west-European terms the *kulak* would have been classified as a modestly well-off farmer.

left communists Bukharin was the leader of this group on the Central Committee (October 1917–18); they favoured the immediate introduction of socialism and a revolutionary war against imperial Germany. Lenin wanted a slow march to socialism and peace with Berlin; he eventually won over a majority of the Central Committee.

Lend-Lease US military and food aid to Allies during the Second World War; authorised by Congress in March 1941 to aid Great Britain, it was extended to include China in April and the USSR in September 1941; about 22 per cent of aid or US$10,000 million went to the Soviet Union.

Mensheviks When the All-Russian Social Democratic Labour Party (RSDRP), founded in 1898, split in 1903, those in the minority became known as Mensheviks; in October 1917 the Mensheviks opposed the Bolshevik seizure of power since they believed that Russia was not ready for socialism; they thought that the country had to become strong economically and a large working class come into being before a socialist revolution became a possibility.

mir Peasant commune.

moderate socialists Mensheviks and right Social Revolutionaries; they were called moderate to contrast them with the radical Bolsheviks.

muzhik Russian peasant.

NEP New Economic Policy, introduced in March 1921; it brought back the market economy with money again being backed by gold; during NEP peasants could dispose of their produce as they liked; light industry also passed into private hands but heavy engineering, energy and transport stayed in state hands; in practice ended in 1929.

NKVD People's Commissariat of Internal Affairs; renamed Ministry of Internal Affairs (MVD) in April 1946.

NSDAP National Socialist German Workers' Party or Nazi Party.

Orgburo Organisational Bureau of the CC; handled all matters of an organisational and administrative nature, domestic and foreign, except those deemed important enough to be passed over to the Politburo; abolished in 1952.

Politburo Political Bureau of the CC; key decision-making body of the Communist Party; established in 1919; prior to that the Central Committee was the most significant body; called the Presidium between 1952 and 1966.

Presidium Inner council or cabinet, hence supreme body; the Politburo of the Communist Party was also known as the Presidium between 1952 and 1966.

Rabkrin People's Commissariat of Workers and Peasants Inspection; founded in 1920 to supervise all government organs; dissolved in 1934 when functions were transferred to Commission of Soviet Control; in 1940 became People's Commissariat of State Control and from 1946 Ministry of State Control. Headed by J.V. Stalin, 1920–22; A.D. Tsyurupa, 1922–23; V.V. Kuibyshev, 1923–26; S. Ordzhonikidze, 1926–30; A.A. Andreev, 1930–34.

RAPP All-Russian Association of Proletarian Writers; founded 1928 and dissolved in 1932; *see also* AUSW and AUW.

RCP All-Russian Communist Party (Bolsheviks) 1918–25; formerly All-Russian Social Democratic Labour Party (RSDRP) 1898–1918; renamed All-Union Communist Party (Bolsheviks) 1925–52; renamed Communist Party of the Soviet Union (CPSU) 1952–91.

Right Opposition Bukharin, Rykov, Tomsky and their supporters came together in the summer of 1928 to oppose the headlong rush towards industrialisation which was then beginning to gain momentum; they favoured voluntary collectivisation which meant in practice very slow collectivisation; by early 1929 they had been defeated by Stalin.

RSFSR Russian Soviet Federated Socialist Republic; constitution adopted July 1918; between October 1917 and July 1918 the state was referred to as Soviet Russia or the Russian republic – in essence it amounted to the

RSFSR; when the USSR was formed in December 1922 the RSFSR became the largest republic; between June 1918 and December 1922 the RSFSR concluded treaties with Belorussia, Ukraine, Georgia, Armenia, Azerbaidzhan and Central Asia – together they formed the Soviet state.

Secretariat The administrative centre of the Communist Party; its key officials were called secretaries and the leading one Secretary-General (1922–53, 1966–) or First Secretary (1953–66); only from 1929 was the Secretary-General the leader of the Soviet Union.

SED Socialist Unity Party; ruling communist party in the German Democratic Republic; founded in April 1946.

Sovkhoz State farm; run like a factory with guaranteed minimum wages higher than those of *kolkhozniks*; operatives were classified as workers and enjoyed their social benefits.

Soviet Name of state – Soviet Union; also elected council.

Sovkhoznik State farm worker; his private plot was smaller than that of a *kolkhoznik*.

Sovnarkom The Council of People's Commissars; the government of Soviet Russia and later of the USSR; it was appointed by the IInd Congress of Soviets in October 1917 and was to be subordinate to it but soon proved stronger; all the members of the first *Sovnarkom* were Bolsheviks and picked by Lenin himself; there was a brief coalition government between December 1917 and March 1918 when some left SRs joined; since March 1918 only Bolsheviks or communists have been commissars or ministers; was renamed USSR Council of Ministers in April 1946; according to the 1936 and 1977 constitutions the government should resign at the end of each legislative period, but this was a mere formality. These constitutions also laid down that each republic and autonomous republic (ASSR) was to elect its own government or Council of Ministers to underline the federal nature of the Soviet state, but in reality the USSR Council of Ministers dominated; *Sovnarkom* was the dominant body in the state while Lenin was well, but it was superseded by the Politburo in 1922. Headed by V.I Lenin, October 1917–January 1924; A.I. Rykov, February 1924– December 1930; V.M. Molotov, December 1930–May 1941; J.V. Stalin, May 1941–March 1953.

SPD Social Democratic Party of Germany; refounded in 1945 and fused with KPD in Soviet Zone of Germany in April 1946 to form SED; *see also* KPD.

SRs Socialist Revolutionaries; the SRs constituted an agrarian socialist party; they had great support among the peasants since they advocated the handing over of the land to the peasants; as agrarian socialists they were not Marxists – they sought to influence and represent the urban working class; the party split in 1917 into right and left SRs, the latter supporting the Bolshevik seizure of power in October 1917; the left SRs joined *Sovnarkom* in December 1917 to form the first coalition government but left after refusing to be associated with the Treaty of Brest-Litovsk signed in March 1918; they then joined the anti-Bolshevik opposition, some even resorting to armed violence; the SR parties were banned in the early 1920s.

state capitalism The economic order in existence between October 1917 and June 1918.

Stavka General Staff of the Red Army and Navy during the Great Patriotic War (1941–45).

Supreme Soviet Set up by 1936 constitution; the USSR Supreme Soviet was bicameral: Soviet of the Union and Soviet of Nationalities; the number of deputies of the former was based on population, while the number of the latter was fixed; the houses were of equal status and often met in joint session; a parliament only in name, the key decisions were taken by the government and the party; the chairman of the presidium of the USSR Supreme Soviet was the president of the country; each republic and autonomous republic had its own Supreme Soviet but they were unicameral.

United Opposition Trotsky, Zinoviev, Kamenev and their supporters combined in the summer of 1926 to form the United Opposition – to oppose socialism in one country and the policy of allowing *kulaks* free rein; they favoured a more rapid growth of industry and more weight to be accorded the world socialist revolution; this opposition was directed essentially against Bukharin and Stalin.

USSR Union of Soviet Socialist Republics

VSNKh (Vesenkha) Supreme Council of the National Economy; founded December 1917 and responsible for the whole economy and state finances; as of June 1918 it became in effect the commissariat of nationalised industry; there were local VSNKh to run industry; during the civil war the main function of VSNKh was to provide the Red Army with war material and clothing; under NEP, factories producing similar products were grouped together in trusts but still managed by VSNKh; in 1924 a VSNKh was created in each republic and made responsible for industry there; VSNKh was headed by N. Osinsky, 1917–18; A.I. Rykov, 1918–20, 1923–24; P.A. Bogdanov, 1921–23; F.E. Dzerzhinsky, 1924–26; V.V. Kuibyshev, 1926–30; S. Ordzhonikidze, 1930–32; then it was divided into the Commissariats of Heavy Industry, Light Industry and the Timber Industry.

war communism The economic order in existence between June 1918 and March 1921.

workers' or food requisition detachments Established in August 1918; they were highly successful in requisitioning grain since they were composed of

workers who desperately needed the food for their urban families and the
army and because they had machine guns. Forced requisitioning lasted
until March 1921.

BIBLIOGRAPHY

This bibliography concentrates mainly on works published since 1980. Those published before 1980 can be found in the first edition of this study. The place of publication is London unless otherwise stated.

GENERAL ACCOUNTS

1 Carr, E.H., *The Russian Revolution from Lenin to Stalin*, Macmillan, Basingstoke, 1979.
2 Hosking, G.A., *A History of the Soviet Union*, rev. edn, Fontana, 1990.
3 Knight, A., *Beria: Stalin's First Lieutenant*, Princeton University Press, Princeton NJ, 1993.
4 Knight, Amy W., *The KGB Police and Politics in the Soviet Union*, Unwin Hyman, 1988.
5 McCauley, M., *The Soviet Union 1917–1991*, 2nd edn, Longman, 1993.
6 Medvedev, R.A., *Let History Judge*, Macmillan, Basingstoke, 1973.
7 Medvedev, R.A., *On Socialist Democracy*, Macmillan, Basingstoke, 1975.
8 Nove, A., *An Economic History of the USSR*, Penguin, Harmondsworth, 1992.
9 Schapiro, L., *Totalitarianism*, Pall Mall, 1972.
10 Schecter, Jerrold L. with Luchkov, Vyacheslav V., trans. and ed., *Khrushchev Remembers, The Glasnost Tapes*, Little, Brown & Co., Boston MA, 1990.
11 Talbott, S., ed. and trans., *Khrushchev Remembers*, Little, Brown & Co., Boston MA, 1971.
12 Talbott, S., ed. and trans., *Khrushchev Remembers, The Last Testament*, Little, Brown & Co., Boston MA, 1974.
13 Taubman, William, ed. and trans., *Khrushchev on Khrushchev, An Inside Account of the Man and His Era, by His son, Sergei Khrushchev*, Little, Brown & Co., Boston MA, 1990.
14 Urban, G.R., *Stalinism, Its Impact on Russia and the World*, Maurice Temple Smith, 1982.

POLITICAL

15 Alexandrov, G.F. et al., *Joseph Stalin: a Short Biography*, Foreign Language Publishing House, Moscow, 1947.

16 Andreyev, C., *Vlasov and the Russian Liberation Movement: Soviet Reality and Emigré Theories*, Cambridge University Press, Cambridge, 1987.

17 Cohen, S.F., *Bukharin and the Bolshevik Revolution: a Political Biography 1888–1938*, Oxford University Press, Oxford, 1980.

18 Conquest, R., *Stalin, Breaker of Nations*, Weidenfeld & Nicolson, 1991.

19 Crowfoot, J. and Harrison, M., 'The USSR Council of Ministers Under Later Stalinism, 1945–1954: Its Production Branch Composition and the Requirements of National Economy and Policy', *Soviet Studies* vol. 42, no. 1, January 1990.

20 Dallin, A., *German Rule in Russia 1941–1945: a Study of Occupation Policies*, 2nd edn, Macmillan, Basingstoke, 1981.

21 de Jonge, A., *Stalin and the Shaping of the Soviet Union*, Morrow, New York, 1986.

22 Dedijer, V., *Tito Speaks*, Weidenfeld & Nicolson, 1953.

23 Deutscher, I., *Stalin: a Political Biography*, 2nd edn, Oxford University Press, Oxford, 1972.

24 Djilas, M., *Conversations with Stalin*, Hart-Davis, 1962.

25 Erickson, J., *The Road to Berlin: Stalin's War with Germany*, Weidenfeld & Nicolson, 1983.

26 Farber, S., *Before Stalinism: The Rise and Fall of Soviet Democracy*, Polity Press, Cambridge, 1990.

27 Gill, G., *Stalinism*, Macmillan, Basingstoke, 1990.

28 Gill, G., *The Origins of the Soviet Political System*, Cambridge University Press, Cambridge, 1990.

29 Ginzburg, E., *Into the Whirlwind*, Penguin, Harmondsworth, 1968.

30 Hahn, W.G., *Postwar Soviet Politics: The Fall of Zhdanov and the Defeat of Moderation 1946–53*, Cornell University Press, Ithaca NY, 1982.

31 Homberger, E. and Briggart, J., *John Reed and the Russian Revolution: Uncollected Articles, Letters and Speeches on Russia, 1917–1920*, Macmillan, Basingstoke, 1992.

32 Knight, A., 'Beria and the Cult of Stalin: Rewriting Transcaucasian Party History', *Soviet Studies*, vol. 43, no. 4, 1991.

33 Lampert, N. and Rittersporn, G., *Stalinism, Its Nature and Aftermath*, Macmillan, Basingstoke, 1992.

34 Laqueur, W., *Stalin: The Glasnost Revelations*, Unwin Hyman, 1990.

35 Linz, S.J., ed., *The Impact of World War II on the Soviet Union*, Rowman & Allanheld, Totowa, 1985.

36 McNeal, R.H., *Stalin: Man and Ruler*, New York University Press, New York, 1990.

37 Mandelstam, N., *Hope Abandoned*, Collins, Harvill, 1971.

38   Mandelstam, N., *Hope Against Hope*, Collins, Harvill, 1974.

39   Merridale, C., *Moscow Politics and the Rise of Stalin: The Communist Party in the Capital 1925–32*, Macmillan, Basingstoke, 1990.

40   Nove, A., *The Stalin Phenomenon*, Weidenfeld & Nicolson, 1993.

41   Orenstein, H.S. ed., *Soviet Documents on the Use of War Experience*: Vol. 1, *The Initial Period*; Vol. 2, *The Winter Campaign 1941–1942*, Frank Cass, 1991.

42   Pomper, P., *Lenin, Trotsky and Stalin: The Intelligentsia and Power*, Columbia University Press, New York, 1990.

43   Rigby, T.H., *Stalin*, Prentice-Hall, Englewood Cliffs NJ, 1966.

44   Rigby, T.H., *The Changing Soviet System: Mono-Organisational Socialism from its Origins to Gorbachev's Restructuring*, Edward Elgar, Cheltenham, 1990.

45   Rittersporn, G., *Stalinist Simplifications and Soviet Complications: Social Tensions and Political Conflicts in the USSR 1933–1953*, Harwood, Chur, 1991.

46   Schulte, T.J., *The German Army and Nazi Policies in Occupied Russia*, Berg, Oxford, 1989.

47   Stalin, J., *Problems of Leninism*, Foreign Language Publishing House, Moscow, 1945.

48   Thorniley, D., *The Rise and Fall of the Soviet Rural Communist Party 1927–39*, Macmillan, Basingstoke, 1988.

49   Trotsky, L., *Stalin: an Appraisal of the Man and His Influence*, Hollis & Carter, 1947.

50   Tucker, R.C., *Stalin in Power: The Revolution from Above 1929–1941*, W.W. Norton, New York, 1990.

51   Tucker, R.C. ed., *Stalinism: Essays in Historical Interpretation*, W.W. Norton, New York, 1977.

52   Ulam, A.B., *Stalin: The Man and His Era*, 2nd edn, Beacon Press, Boston MA, 1989.

53   Volkogonov, D., *Stalin: Triumph and Tragedy*, trans. H. Shukman, Weidenfeld & Nicolson, 1991.

54   von Laue, T.H., 'Stalin Among the Moral and Political Imperatives, or How to Judge Stalin', *Soviet Union/Union Soviétique*, vol. 8, no. 1, 1981.

55   von Laue, T.H., 'Stalin in Focus', *Slavic Review*, vol. 10, no. 3, 1983.

56   von Laue, T.H., 'Stalin Reviewed', *Soviet Union/Union Soviétique*, vol. 11, no. 1, 1984.

57   Ward, C., *Stalin's Russia*, Edward Arnold, 1993.

ECONOMIC AND SOCIAL

58   Andrle, V., *Workers in Stalin's Russia: Industrialization and Social Change in a Planned Economy*, Harvester/Wheatsheaf, Hemel Hempstead, 1988.

59   Atkinson, D., *The End of the Russian Land Commune 1905–1930*, Stanford University Press, Stanford CA, 1983.

60   Atkinson, D., Dallin, A. and Lapidus, G.W. eds, *Women in Russia*, Stanford University Press, Stanford CA, 1977.

61   Bacon, E., '*Glasnost* and the Gulag: New Information on Soviet Forced Labour around World War II', *Soviet Studies*, vol. 44, no. 6, 1992.

62   Barber, J.D. and Harrison, M., *The Soviet Home Front 1941–1945: a Social and Economic History of the USSR in World War II*, Longman, 1991.

63   Chase, W.J., *Workers, Society and the Soviet State: Labour and Life in Moscow 1918–1929*, University of Illinois Press, Champaign IL, 1987.

64   Conquest, R., *The Harvest of Sorrow: Soviet Collectivization and the Terror-Famine*, Hutchinson, 1986.

65   Dalrymple, D.G., 'The Soviet famine of 1932-1934', *Soviet Studies*, vol. 16, no. 3, 1964.

66   Danilov, V.P., *Rural Russia under the New Regime*, ed. O. Figes, Hutchinson, 1988.

67   Davies, R.W. ed., *From Tsarism to New Economic Policy: Continuity and Change in the Economy of the USSR*, Macmillan, Basingstoke, 1990.

68   Davies, R.W., 'Soviet Military Expenditure and the Armaments Industry, 1929–33: A Reconsideration', *Europe-Asia Studies*, vol. 45, no. 4, 1993.

69   Davies, R.W., *The Industrialisation of Soviet Russia*, Vol. 1: *The Socialist Offensive: The Collectivisation of Soviet Agriculture 1929–30*, Macmillan, 1980; Vol. 2: *The Soviet Collective Farm*, Macmillan, 1980; Vol. 3: *The Soviet Economy in Turmoil 1929–30*, Macmillan, Basingstoke, 1989.

70   Davies, R.W., Harrison, M. and Wheatcroft, S.G. eds, *The Economic Transformation of the Soviet Union 1913–1945*, Cambridge University Press, Cambridge, 1994.

71   Dunmore, T., *The Stalinist Command Economy: The Soviet State Apparatus and Economic Policy, 1945–53*, Macmillan, Basingstoke, 1980.

72   Ellman, M., 'A Note on the Number of 1933 Famine Victims', *Soviet Studies*, vol. 43, no. 2, 1991.

73   Ellman, M. and Maksudov, S., 'Soviet Deaths in the Great Patriotic War: A Note', *Europe-Asia Studies*, vol. 46, no. 4, 1994.

74   Figes, O., *Peasant Russia, Civil War: The Volga Countryside in Revolution 1917–1921*, Oxford University Press, Oxford, 1989.

75   Filtzer, D., *Soviet Workers and Stalinist Industrialization: The Formation of Modern Soviet Production Relations*, Pluto Press, 1986.

76   Garrard, J. and C. eds, *World War 2 and the Soviet People: Selected Papers from the IV World Congress for SEES, Harrogate 1990*, St Martin's Press, New York, 1993.

77 Gelb, M. ed., *An American Engineer in Stalin's Russia: The Memoirs of Zara Witkin, 1932–1934*, University of California Press, Berkeley CA, 1991.

78 Getty, J.A., *Origins of the Great Purges: The Soviet Communist Party Reconsidered, 1933–1938*, Cambridge University Press, Cambridge, 1985.

79 Getty, J.A. and Manning, R.T. eds, *Stalinist Terror: New Perspectives*, Cambridge University Press, Cambridge, 1993.

80 Goldman, W.Z., *Women, the State and Revolution: Soviet Family Policy and Social Life, 1917–1936*, Cambridge University Press, Cambridge, 1993.

81 Harrison, M., 'Soviet Economic Growth Since 1928: The Alternative Statistics of G.I. Khanin', *Europe-Asia Studies*, vol. 45, no. 1, 1993.

82 Harrison, M., *Soviet Planning in Peace and War 1938–1945*, Cambridge University Press, Cambridge, 1985.

83 Hoffman, David L., 'Land, Freedom and Discontent: Russian Peasants of the Central Industrial Region Prior to Collectivization', *Europe-Asia Studies*, vol. 46, no. 4, 1994.

84 Hughes, J., *Stalin, Siberia and the Crisis of the New Economic Policy*, Cambridge University Press, Cambridge, 1991.

85 Hunter, H. and Szyrmer, J.M., *Faulty Foundations: Soviet Economic Policies, 1928–1940*, Princeton University Press, Princeton NJ, 1992.

86 Jasny, N., *Soviet Industrialization 1928–1952*, University of Chicago Press, Chicago IL, 1981.

87 Karasev, I.V., 'The Reconstruction of Agriculture in Pskov *Oblast* 1945–1953', *Soviet Studies*, vol. 43, no. 2, 1991.

88 Kirsch, L.J., *Soviet Wages*, MIT Press, Cambridge MA, 1972.

89 Kuromiya, H., *Stalin's Industrial Revolution: Politics and Workers 1928–1932*, Cambridge University Press, Cambridge, 1988.

90 Lewin, M., *The Making of the Soviet System: Essays on the Social History of Inter-war Russia*, Methuen, 1985.

91 Lih, L.T., *Bread and Authority in Russia 1914–1921*, University of California Press, Berkeley CA, 1990.

92 Medvedev, Z.A., *Soviet Agriculture*, W.W. Norton, New York, 1987.

93 Miller, J.R., *The Soviet Economic Experiment*, ed. S.J. Linz, University of Illinois Press, Champaign IL, 1990.

94 Moskoff, W., *The Bread of Affliction: The Food Supply in the USSR during World War II*, Cambridge University Press, Cambridge, 1990.

95 Preobrazhenskii, E., *The Crisis of Soviet Industrialization. Selected Essays*, ed. D. Filtzer, Macmillan, Basingstoke, 1980.

96 Rassweiler, A.D., *The Generation of Power: The History of Dneprostroi*, Oxford University Press, Oxford, 1988.

97 Salter, J., 'On the Interpretation of Bukharin's Economic Ideas', *Soviet Studies*, vol. 44, no. 4, 1992.

98 Siegelbaum, L.H., *Soviet State and Society Between Revolutions, 1918–1929*, Cambridge University Press, Cambridge, 1992.

99   Siegelbaum, L.H., *Stakhanovism and the Politics of Productivity in the USSR 1935–1941*, Cambridge University Press, Cambridge, 1988.

100   Solnick, S.L., 'Revolution, Reform and the Soviet Telephone System, 1919–1927', *Soviet Studies*, vol. 43, no. 1, 1991.

101   Viola, L., *The Best Sons of the Fatherland: Workers in the Vanguard of Collectivization*, Oxford University Press, Oxford, 1987.

102   Ward, C., *Russia's Cotton Workers and the New Economic Policy: Shopfloor Culture and State Policy 1921–29*, Cambridge University Press, Cambridge, 1990.

103   Wheatcroft, S.G., 'More Light on the Scale of Repression and Excess Mortality in the Soviet Union in the 1930s', *Soviet Studies*, vol. 42, no. 2, 1990.

104   Wheatcroft, S.G. and Davies R.W., *Materials for a Balance of Soviet National Economy 1928–1930*, Cambridge University Press, Cambridge, 1985.

105   Zaleski, E., *Stalinist Planning for Economic Growth 1933–1952*, Macmillan, Basingstoke, 1980.

LEGAL

106   Benvenuti, F., 'Industry and Purge in the Donbass, 1936–37', *Europe-Asia Studies*, vol. 45, no. 1, 1993.

107   Conquest, R., *Stalin and the Kirov Murder*, Hutchinson, 1989.

108   Conquest, R., *The Great Terror: A Reassessment*, Hutchinson, 1990.

109   *Jahrbuch für Historische Kommunismusforschung 1993*, Akademie Verlag, Berlin, 1993.

110   Rittersporn, G., 'Soviet Officialdom and Political Evolution. Judiciary Apparatus and Penal Policy in the 1930s', *Theory and Society*, vol. 11, no. 2, 1984.

111   Scherer, J.L. and Jakobson, M., 'The Collectivisation of Agriculture and the Soviet Prison Camp System', *Europe-Asia Studies*, vol. 45, no. 3, 1993.

112   Solomon, P.H., 'Soviet Penal Policy 1917–1934: a Reconsideration', *Slavic Review*, xxxix, no. 2, 1980.

113   Solomon, P.H., 'Local Political Power and Soviet Criminal Justice 1922–41', *Soviet Studies*, vol. 37, no. 3, 1985.

114   Wimberg, E., 'Socialism, Democratism and Criticism: The Soviet Press and the National Discussion of the 1936 Draft Constitution', *Soviet Studies*, vol. 44, no. 2, 1992.

NATIONALITIES

115   Carrere D'Encausse, H., *The Great Challenge: Nationalities and the Bolshevik State 1917–1930*, Holmes and Meier, New York, 1992.

116 Davies, N. and Polonsky, A., *Jews in Eastern Poland and the USSR, 1939–46*, Macmillan, Basingstoke, 1991.

117 Forsyth, J., *A History of the Peoples of Siberia: Russia's North Asian Colony 1581–1990*, Cambridge University Press, Cambridge, 1992.

118 Gilboa, Y.A., *The Black Years of Soviet Jewry 1939–53*, Little, Brown & Co., Boston MA, 1971.

119 Marples, D.R., *Stalinism in Ukraine in the 1940s*, St Martin's Press, New York, 1992.

120 Simon, G., *Nationalism and Policy Toward the Nationalities in the Soviet Union: From Totalitarian Dictatorship to Post-Stalinist Society*, Westview Press, Boulder CO, 1991.

121 Sword, K. ed., *The Soviet Takeover of the Polish Eastern Provinces, 1939–41*, Macmillan, Basingstoke, 1991.

CULTURAL

122 Barber, J., *Soviet Historians in Crisis 1928–32*, Macmillan, Basingstoke, 1981.

123 Bown, M.C., *Art Under Stalin*, Holmes and Meier, New York, 1991.

124 Clark, K., *The Soviet Novel: History as Ritual*, University of Chicago Press, Chicago IL, 1981.

125 Fitzpatrick, S., *The Cultural Front: Power and Culture in Revolutionary Russia*, Cornell University Press, Ithaca NY, 1992.

126 Fitzpatrick, S., 'New Perspectives on Stalinism', *The Russian Review*, vol. 45, 1986.

127 Fitzpatrick, S., Rabinowitch, A. and Stites, R., *Russia in the Era of NEP: Explorations in Soviet Society and Culture*, Indiana University Press, Bloomington IN, 1991.

128 Gleason, A., *et al.* eds, *Bolshevik Culture: Experiment and Order in the Russian Revolution*, Indiana University Press, Bloomington IN, 1985.

129 Fox, M.S, 'Glavlit, Censorship and the Problem of Party Policy in Cultural Affairs, 1922–28', *Europe-Asia Studies*, vol. 44, no. 6, 1992.

130 Goodwin, J., *Eisenstein, Cinema, and History*, University of Illinois Press, Champaign IL, 1993.

131 Graham, L.R. ed., *Science and the Soviet Social Order*, Harvard University Press, Cambridge MA, 1990.

132 Graham, L.R., *Science in Russia and the Soviet Union: a Short History*, Cambridge University Press, Cambridge, 1993.

133 Günther, H. ed., *The Culture of the Stalin Period*, Macmillan, Basingstoke, 1990.

134 Josephson, P.R., *Physics and Politics in Revolutionary Russia*, University of California Press, Berkeley CA, 1991.

135 Kemp-Welch, A., *Stalin and the Literary Intelligentsia, 1928–1939*, Macmillan, Basingstoke, 1991.

136   Kenez, P., *Cinema and Soviet Society 1917–1953*, Cambridge
       University Press, Cambridge, 1992.

137   Muckle, J., *Education in Russia Past and Present: an Introductory
       Study Guide and Select Bibliography*, Bramcote Press, Nottingham,
       1993.

138   Norman, Baer van Nancy, ed., *Russian Avant-Garde Stage Design,
       1913–1935*, Thames and Hudson, 1991.

139   Peris, D., 'The 1929 Congress of the Godless', *Soviet Studies*, vol. 43,
       no. 4, 1991.

140   Raeff, M., *Russians Abroad: a Cultural History of the Russian
       Emigration 1919–1939*, Oxford University Press, Oxford, 1990.

141   Robin, R., *Socialist Realism: an Impossible Aesthetic*, Stanford
       University Press, Stanford CA, 1992.

142   Sapiets, M., *True Witness, The Story of Seventh Day Adventists in
       the Soviet Union*, Keston College, Bromley, 1990.

143   Scatton, L.H., *Michael Zoshchenko: Evolution of a Writer*,
       Cambridge University Press, Cambridge, 1993.

144   Stites, R., *Revolutionary Dreams: Utopian Vision and Experimental
       Life in the Russian Revolution*, Oxford University Press, Oxford,
       1989.

145   Stites, R., *Russian Popular Culture: Entertainment and Society since
       1900*, Cambridge University Press, Cambridge, 1992.

146   Strong, J.W. ed., *Essays on Revolutionary Culture and Stalinism:
       Selected Papers from the Third World Congress for Soviet and East
       European Studies*, Slavica, Columbus OH, 1990.

147   Thurston, R.W., 'The Soviet Family During the Great Terror
       1935–41', *Soviet Studies*, vol. 43, no. 3, 1991.

148   Waters, E., 'The Modernisation of Russian Motherhood,
       1917–1937', *Soviet Studies*, vol. 44, no. 1, 1992.

149   Youngblood, D.J., *Movies for the Masses: Popular Cinema and
       Soviet Society in the 1920s*, Cambridge University Press,
       Cambridge, 1992.

FOREIGN POLICY

150   Carley, M.J., 'End of the "Low, Dishonest Decade": Failure of the
       Anglo-Franco-Soviet Alliance in 1939', *Europe-Asia Studies*, vol.
       45, no. 2, 1993.

151   Carr, E.H., *The Twilight of the Comintern 1930–1935*, Macmillan,
       Basingstoke, 1982.

152   Debo, R.K., *Survival and Consolidation: The Foreign Policy of Soviet
       Russia 1918–1921*, McGill-Queen's University Press, Montreal,
       1992.

153   Haslam, J., *Soviet Foreign Policy 1930–33: The Impact of the Great
       Depression*, Macmillan, Basingstoke, 1982.

154 Haslam, J., *The Soviet Union and the Struggle for Collective Security in Europe 1933–39*, Macmillan, Basingstoke, 1984.

155 Low, A.D., 'The Soviet Union, The Austrian Communist Party and the Anschluss Question 1918–1938', *Slavic Studies*, xxxix, no. 1, 1980.

156 Miner, S.M., *Between Stalin and Churchill: The Soviet Union, Great Britain and the Origins of the Grand Alliance*, University of North Carolina Press, Chapel Hill NC, 1988.

157 Read, A., *The Deadly Embrace: Hitler, Stalin and the Nazi-Soviet Pact 1939–1941*, Joseph, 1986.

158 Roberts, G., 'The Soviet Decision for a Pact with Nazi Germany', *Soviet Studies*, vol. 44, no. 1, 1992.

159 *Soviet Foreign Policy During the Patriotic War: Documents and Materials*, vol. 1, June 22, 1941–December 31, 1943, Hutchinson, n.d.

160 Yergin, D., *Shattered Peace: The Origins of the Cold War and the National Security State*, Penguin, Harmondsworth, 1980.

INDEX

RELATED TITLES

Anthony Wood, *The Russian Revolution*
Second Edition (1986)   0 582 35559 1

This study provides a concise history of the Revolution and analyses the relationship between the various social theories of the revolutionaries and the later course of events. It traces the heated arguments amongst left-wing groups from the years before the fall of the monarchy up to the propounding of the New Economic Policy by Lenin in 1921, and concludes by considering why the Bolsheviks succeeded in seizing and retaining power.

John Hiden, *The Weimar Republic*
Second Edition (1996)   0 582 28706 5

It is usually assumed that, thanks to the harsh terms of the Versailles Settlement, the Weimar Republic was doomed from the outset and that Hitler's rise to power was inevitable. In this succinct *Seminar Study* (now revised for the first time since 1974) Professor Hiden seeks to dispel this simplistic view. He examines the fundamental problems of the new state but also argues that it did make some progress in tackling the major political, social and economic problems facing it in the 1920s. The author concludes by showing how it was a complex interaction of many factors which finally brought Hitler to power.

D G Williamson, *The Third Reich*
Second Edition (1995)   0 582 20914 5

Revised and expanded, the Second Edition of this highly successful *Seminar Study* introduces readers to the historical phenomenon of Hitler's Third Reich. The new edition includes two brand new chapters, one on Nazi policy towards the Jews between 1933 and 1939 and one on the Holocaust itself. Fully updated, the study remains as useful and as thought-provoking as ever.

Harry Browne, *Spain's Civil War*
Second Edition (1996)   0 582 28988 2

Harry Browne's accessible account of the Spanish Civil War has now been updated, and expanded, in the light of recent scholarship. In particular, there is now a fuller analysis of the politics of the Second Republic and the regional and social bases of Spain's political parties. There is also a more detailed account of the military conduct of the war, of the extent of international involvement, and of the means by which both sides, despite the Non-Intervention Agreement, were able to purchase arms abroad.

R J Overy, *The Origins of the Second World War*
(1987)   0 582 35378 5

The Second World War has usually been seen simply as Hitler's war. Yet the conflict that broke out in September 1939 was not the war that Hitler wanted. He had hoped for a short war against Poland; instead, Britain and France declared war on Germany. Any explanation of the outbreak of hostilities must therefore be multi-national, examining British and French motives alongside those of Hitler's Germany. It was, after all, Britain and France who declared war on Germany not the other way round; and, as Richard Overy stresses in his hugely successful *Seminar Study*, their policy, like Germany's, was governed primarily by reasons of state, and only secondarily by moral considerations.

Martin McCauley, *The Origins of the Cold War 1941-1949*
Second Edition (1995)   0 582 27659 4

This popular study explores the key questions facing students. Who was responsible for the Cold War? Was it inevitable? Was Stalin genuinely interested in a post-war agreement? For the Second Edition Martin McCauley has revised and expanded his original text in the light of recent events - the ending of the Cold War, the collapse of Communism and the demise of the USSR in 1991.

Martin McCauley, *The Khrushchev Era, 1953-1964*
(1995)   0 582 27776 0

In this new study Martin McCauley explores all aspects of the Khrushchev era: including reforms in agriculture, economic policy, uprisings in Eastern Europe, the Cuban Missile Crisis of 1962, de-Stalinisation and Khrushchev's attempts to reform the Communist Party. The book will be greatly welcomed by history and politics alike.

School of Academic Studies

Croydon College
Fairfield
Croydon CR9 1DX
0181 686 5700

CROYDON
COLLEGE